JOYCE

TTRIDGE

Granta Books

London

For Jacques Berthoud
. . . maestro di color che sanno

Granta Publications, 2/3 Hanover Yard, Noel Road, London N1 8BE

First published in Great Britain by Granta Books 2007

A CIP catalogue record for this book is
available from the British Library.

1 3 5 7 9 10 8 6 4 2

ISBN 978–1–86207–912–0

Typeset by M Rules

Printed and bound in Great Britain by
Bookmarque Limited, Croydon, Surrey

CONTENTS

SERIES EDITOR'S FOREWORD

How am I to read *How to Read*?

This series is based on a very simple, but novel idea. Most beginners' guides to great thinkers and writers offer either a potted biography or condensed summaries of their major works, or perhaps even both. *How to Read*, by contrast, brings the reader face-to-face with the writing itself in the company of an expert guide. Its starting point is that in order to get close to what a writer is all about, you have to get close to the words they actually use and be shown how to read those words.

Every book in the series is in a way a masterclass in reading. Each author has selected ten or so short extracts from a writer's work and looks at them in detail as a way of revealing their central ideas and thereby opening doors onto a whole world of thought. Sometimes these extracts are arranged chronologically to give a sense of a thinker's development over time, sometimes not. The books are not merely compilations of a thinker's most famous passages, their 'greatest hits', but rather they offer a series of clues or keys that will enable readers to go on and make discoveries of their own. In addition to the texts and readings, each book provides a short biographical chronology and suggestions for further reading, Internet resources, and so on. The books in the *How to Read* series don't claim to tell you all you need to know about

Freud, Nietzsche and Darwin, or indeed Shakespeare and the Marquis de Sade, but they do offer the best starting point for further exploration.

Unlike the available second-hand versions of the minds that have shaped our intellectual, cultural, religious, political and scientific landscape, *How to Read* offers a refreshing set of first-hand encounters with those minds. Our hope is that these books will, by turn, instruct, intrigue, embolden, encourage and delight.

Simon Critchley
New School for Social Research, New York

A NOTE ON JOYCE'S TEXTS

Joyce's works are available in a number of editions; the following comments may help in choosing which to buy or borrow. For editions that are particularly valuable for their annotations, see 'Suggestions for Further Reading' at the end of this book.

Dubliners. Page references in this book are to the text edited by Hans Walter Gabler, published as a Vintage paperback (New York: Random House, 1993). There are no major differences between the various texts, however, so other editions pose no significant problems.

A Portrait of the Artist as a Young Man. The Vintage paperback edited by Hans Walter Gabler (New York: Random House, 1993) offers a scrupulously edited text, and is the source of page references in this book. This is also the text used in the Norton Critical Edition, edited by John Paul Riquelme (2006). The other annotated editions mentioned in 'Suggestions for Further Reading' are also acceptable, though there are some differences in the text.

Ulysses. The many errors of the original publication have given rise to some acrimonious debates about how they should be corrected, but the common consensus among Joyce scholars is that the edition first published in 1984 with left-hand pages indicating Joyce's manuscript revisions, edited by Hans Walter Gabler with Wolfhard Steppe and Claus Melchior, resulted in the best reading text. This text is published in paperback in the United States by Vintage (1986) and in the United Kingdom by The Bodley Head (1993). *Ulysses* references in this book are to this edition, and take the form of episode number followed by line numbers, e.g. 18.1128–9. Most critical studies of Joyce since the mid-1980s refer to this edition. Earlier texts still available, which may be more pleasant to read although they contain more errors, are the 1960 Bodley Head edition and the 1961 Random House edition, both reprinted many times. Penguin brought out a new edition in 1968, but this had as many errors as its predecessors.

Finnegans Wake. The text has never been re-edited, so all editions are essentially the same. Choose one with a large-page format for ease of annotation! There are two good-sized Penguin editions, the British one with an introduction by Seamus Deane (1992), the American one with an introduction by John Bishop (1999), both to be recommended. References are in the form of page number and line number, e.g. 112.03.

INTRODUCTION

When Margaret Anderson and Jane Heap started serializing the chapters of Joyce's unpublished novel *Ulysses* in their magazine *The Little Review* they received, according to Anderson, hundreds of complaints from readers. The following was typical:

> I think this is the most damnable slush and filth that ever polluted paper in print ... Damnable, hellish filth from the gutter of a human mind born and bred in contamination. There are no words I know to describe, even vaguely, how disgusted I am; not with the mire of his effusion but with all those whose minds are so putrid that they dare allow such muck and sewage of the human mind to besmirch the world by repeating it.[1]

The appearance of the whole work in 1922 – published by a small bookshop in Paris when no established publishing house would touch it – evoked similar responses. Sewers were often mentioned, mostly in reference to the last chapter, where Joyce's leading lady, Molly Bloom, expresses her thoughts without censorship. 'The whole thing is a hodgepodge of type,' wrote one reviewer of this chapter, 'closely run together, mostly without sense, difficult to read, and flowing on to the end of the book, like a sewer that had burst loose and overwhelmed a city with foul and pestilential vapors.'[2] A few people had particular cause for complaint, as Joyce had

based many of his characters on easily recognizable Dublin
figures, such as his erstwhile companion Oliver St John Gogarty
(who found himself thinly disguised as the joker of the novel,
Malachi Mulligan). Gogarty complained angrily, 'That bloody
Joyce whom I kept in my youth has written a book you can
read on all the lavatory walls of Dublin.'[3]

What is curious about the heated reaction to *Ulysses* on its
publication is the way in which the anger ostensibly directed
at the book's obscenity often seems to implicate another,
apparently unrelated, target: its difficulty. Joyce developed a
style to represent the fragmentariness of thoughts, shifting
from one mode to another between chapters, casting one
episode as a series of stylistic pastiches, another as an unper-
formable play, another as a bizarre catechism (to name just a
few of his innovations). Why should so many people have
found his experiments with the language and structure of the
traditional novel offensive rather than just peculiar?

The answer has to do with expectations. Just as readers in
1922 did not expect to encounter certain words and certain
human experiences in print – or not in respectable publications, at any rate – they did not expect to find fictional events
and characters presented to them in language that seemed
to have a life of its own instead of serving the purposes of
description and narrative. (It didn't help that this challenging
prose went on for over 700 large-format pages.) Shane Leslie,
reviewing *Ulysses* on its publication, was not alone in believ-
ing that 'a gigantic effort has been made to fool the world
of readers'.[4] Seventeen years later when Joyce published
Finnegans Wake, which took even more liberties with the
conventions of the novel and the English language, the outcry
about its difficulty far surpassed reactions to its challenging of
sexual taboos. After the early publication of some sections
of the work, then known only as *Work in Progress*, H. G. Wells
wrote to Joyce, 'You have turned your back on common

men, on their elementary needs and their restricted time and intelligence and you have elaborated. What is the result? Vast riddles.'[5]

But Joyce also had some staunch and influential defenders, who started the process that was eventually to take him to the pinnacle of the literary canon. T. S. Eliot wrote an influential review praising *Ulysses* as having 'the importance of a scientific discovery'; Ezra Pound was tireless in promoting the book; and W. B. Yeats wrote that in *Ulysses* Joyce had 'surpassed in intensity any novelist of our time' (though he later admitted he had not been able to finish it). And Joyce was not above engineering his own critical reception. He helped his friend Stuart Gilbert finish and publish *James Joyce's Ulysses* (1930), which became a foundational study of the Homeric dimension of his modern epic, as well as enabling readers who couldn't get their hands on *Ulysses* – which was banned in many countries – to enjoy a taste of its contents. He suggested that another friend, Frank Budgen, write a book on *Ulysses*, based partly on their many conversations in Zurich; Budgen agreed, and *James Joyce and the Making of 'Ulysses'* was published in 1934. And he both initiated and took a strong interest in the first biographical study, Herbert Gorman's *James Joyce*, published in 1939. Similarly, to help pave the way for *Finnegans Wake*, he organized a collection of critical essays under the Wakean title, *Our Exagmination round His Factification for Incamination of Work in Progress*, which appeared in 1929, ten years before the book itself. Of these twelve essays, the one that has best survived the test of time was by a young admirer named Samuel Beckett.

Although Joyce never visited America, it was there that his reputation in the academic world was well and truly launched. The influential critic Edmund Wilson was a strong supporter of Joyce's work, writing important articles on *Ulysses* (in 1929) and *Finnegans Wake* (in 1939, the year it was published). Joyce

suggested to the New Directions Press that a young scholar of
Elizabethan drama, Harry Levin, be invited to write a book
on all his work, and Levin's pioneering *James Joyce* (1941)
remains one of the best introductions to Joyce today. Joseph
Campbell and Henry Morton Robinson gave would-be readers of *Finnegans Wake* a route through the thickets of the text
with their 1944 *Skeleton Key*. A number of other American
scholars published work on Joyce in the 1940s and 1950s,
including Richard M. Kain and Hugh Kenner, and Joyce's
stature as one of the great twentieth-century writers was
secured with the appearance of Richard Ellmann's imposing
but highly readable biography in 1959. The rise of formalist
criticism in North American universities provided classroom
techniques that made possible the close consideration of
Joyce's carefully crafted language, and his writing became a
staple of the school and university curriculum.

Outside North America, there were louder voices against
Joyce in the years after his death in 1941. The most influential British critic of the mid-twentieth century, F. R. Leavis,
pronounced *Ulysses* 'a dead end', and had no time for *Finnegans
Wake*, while in his native country Joyce provoked as much
dismay as admiration for a considerable period. Ken Monaghan,
a nephew of Joyce's who grew up in Dublin, tells how he was
advised by his family not to admit to having any connection
with the scandalous author. It was left to the creative responses
by Irish writers such as Flann O'Brien and Beckett to honour
Joyce's achievement, though in Beckett's case it was from outside the country.

Despite these opposing voices, by the 1960s Joyce was
securely installed as one of the central figures, perhaps *the*
central figure, in what had come to be called modernist literature, which embraced a number of writers of the period
between the two world wars, including Franz Kafka, William
Faulkner, Marcel Proust, T. S. Eliot, Gertrude Stein, Thomas

Mann, Virginia Woolf, Wallace Stevens and Luigi Pirandello. As well as writers, of course, the modernist movement embraced painters and sculptors, composers, theatre and film directors, and a variety of other creative artists. It was a thoroughly international movement, and Joyce's residence in several European countries and facility in a number of languages were an important part of his modernist identity. *Ulysses*, in particular, became a benchmark for 'high modernism': the unapologetic pursuit of virtuoso techniques designed to capture the full breadth of human experience in the early twentieth century, willing to risk the fate of being read only by a minority.

Partly because he was such a European figure, Joyce's reputation remained high on the Continent, and it was from France that a fresh breeze of Joycean appreciation was to blow in the 1970s and 1980s, thanks to the significant part his work had played in the intellectual formation of such thinkers as Jacques Derrida, Jacques Lacan, Julia Kristeva and Hélène Cixous. The later growth of more historically based studies, together with the huge interest in post-colonial writing, resulted in another new wave of Joyce studies towards the end of the century, now with Irish scholars playing a full part. By this time, the phrase 'the Joyce industry' was frequently to be heard, and contained a good deal of truth. Massive sales, top billing in media polls, an International James Joyce Foundation, biennial international conferences (and numerous smaller ones), films, journals, and an ever-mounting quantity of secondary works testified to his extraordinary reputation, a reputation that shows no signs of diminishing in the twenty-first century.

Today, our expectations about what can or should be put in print are very different from those of 1922. The explicitness with which Joyce treated sex and bodily functions is no longer shocking. But *Ulysses* is still widely perceived as a difficult book, a book for academics or anoraks, a book that requires too much hard work for too little pay-off in enjoyment. As for *Finnegans Wake* — even the academics and anoraks tend to agree with the common reader that its demands are just too great for whatever pleasures it might hold in store. Yet those early readers of *Ulysses* who, perhaps unconsciously, linked the book's frankness about sex and the body with its difficulty were not simply confusing two different sources of irritation and bewilderment. The unprecedented completeness with which Joyce wished to transcribe the mental processes of his characters required a technique that challenged the ortho-doxies of traditional prose, and when his aim was to parody his predecessors, make fun of the conventions of the novel, or do justice to the unconscious mental processes that manifest themselves in dreams and fantasies, his departure from those orthodoxies would inevitably be even more marked.

In other words, the difficulty of Joyce's last two books — which occupied the last thirty years of his life — is inseparable from their achievement in expanding the reach of the novel to explore hitherto untapped realms of human experience and cultural history. Joyce took the huge risk of asking his readers to follow him in testing language's ability to capture more of our daily existence than any other writer had attempted, and doing so while engaged in a comic raid on his literary heritage. It was a venture that nearly failed, as it ran up against the vari-ous economies and institutions that control the production and dissemination of books — including the market, the church, the state, and the predilections and habits of readers. After *Ulysses*, novelists (in any language) found available to them the means to explore thoughts, feelings, impulses and actions that had until then been inaccessible; and the aftershocks of Joyce's break-through can be felt in many other media — in popular as well as elite culture — all around us today.

However, the expectations that Joyce challenged have not been consigned to the past: the vast majority of the novels we read and films we see still conform to the norms of narrative, character and style that were dominant a hundred years ago, and to encounter *Ulysses* or *Finnegans Wake* for the first time is, for most readers, an unsettling experience. The conventions of realism, established in the nineteenth century, have proved extremely tenacious: we still think of a 'normal' novel or movie as one in which the techniques employed seem transparent and the characters and events appear to have their own independent existence. In fact, of course, the illusion of reality depends on a number of technical devices that we take for granted, such as a clearly defined narrator, whether omniscient or first-person, a series of events conforming to a familiar plot line, and a chronological sequence from a recognizable beginning to a satisfying end. But because we take them for granted, we don't even think of them as conventional techniques.

We must not think of this persistence of traditional forms as a disadvantage; on the contrary, the fullest enjoyment of Joyce's work depends on an awareness that language is being made to do things we are not used to seeing it do, taking us to unfamiliar but exciting places. And one of the paradoxes of Joyce's writing is that because his drive to render more of human experience vivid in language is at the same time a drive to exploit to the full the possibilities of language, our enjoyment of what is being represented in words is inseparable from our enjoyment of the play of the words themselves. Other writers have developed complex styles to capture the subtleties of thought and feeling, or the multifaceted character of modern life, or the fine grain of the historical record, but most of them have put their language at the service of faithful representation. Joyce, on the other hand, revelled in the sheer variety and creative potential of language itself – the language we speak, hear, write and read, but also the language we think in. So to read a work of Joyce's only for the events, places and people it depicts is to miss a great deal of what it has to offer; one might as well read one of the many available summaries of his plots. The instantly gripping quality in Joyce's works is what is going on in the language, sentence by sentence – the moulding of sound in its relation to sense, the play of irony, the echoes of other styles, the resonances within and between chapters and books, the verbal jokes, the condensation of ideas in invented words, the capturing of the trivialities of speech and thought.

One can think of Joyce's achievement in terms of *richness*: every page of his major works has more to offer than can be appreciated in a single reading. This is why Joyce's writing is so rewarding when re-read, or when read in a group; it is also why it seems, compared to most other fiction, 'difficult'. It is not qualitatively different from other works of literature, however; all powerful literature requires a more attentive and open-minded approach than we give to workaday prose, and what Joyce's writing demands is nothing more than a good measure of this attentiveness and open-mindedness. Although Joyce's works grew longer and longer, his care over details never flagged; in fact, the later the work, the more each sentence contains, and the more pleasure there is in relishing the varied facets of the tiniest verbal element.

In the annoyance of earlier reviewers of *Ulysses* it is possible to sense a resentment that a book of over 700 pages isn't an easy read; had it been fifty or a hundred pages long they might have been more willing to give each paragraph the attention it deserves. Faced with the demands of time Joyce's longer books make on the reader it helps to remember how long he laboured over them, and to be aware of the multiple notebooks and drafts that lie behind *Ulysses* and *Finnegans Wake*, many of whose chapters are the equivalent of a short book. This doesn't mean that it is only worth tackling these later books if you have a six-month holiday; there is a great deal to enjoy in reading short extracts. When you feel you are missing references or have not appreciated the full significance of the language, it doesn't follow that you are failing as a reader; rather, it assures you that many pleasures lie in store when you return to individual episodes and tackle them more slowly, perhaps with some of the published guides at your elbow.

In raising the issue of Joyce's difficulty here, I have concentrated on his last two works, and the bulk of the chapters that follow do the same. The reason is obvious: Joyce's two earlier works, the collection of short stories entitled *Dubliners* (published in 1914 but written much earlier) and the semi-autobiographical novel *A Portrait of the Artist as a Young Man* (published as a book in 1916), don't pose the same kind of challenge to the reader. (I have left out of consideration the works that most readers don't come across, including the play *Exiles*, the poems, and two that were unpublished in his lifetime, the novel-fragment *Stephen Hero* and the short poetic fiction *Giacomo Joyce*.) *Dubliners* and *A Portrait* are, however, works which amply repay a similar alertness to detail, since Joyce was by no means writing traditional fiction, as the early reviews once again reveal. In *Dubliners* the simple style itself is deceptive, as a number of commentators have shown; and in *A Portrait* Joyce develops techniques for the representation of a boy's growing consciousness that mark a new stage in the English novel and pave the way for the stylistic adventures of *Ulysses*.

The discussions of short passages that follow will give the reader first-hand experience of what it means to engage with Joyce's writing. Without an alertness to the words and sentences, to their sounds, their meanings, their echoes and foreshadowings, their patterns and relationships, no wider understanding of these works is possible. Only with attentive reading can larger patterns be discerned, political and ethical commitments traced, and connections with broader historical issues and events examined. Although he lived out of Ireland for most of his life, Joyce remained deeply caught up in the political and religious goings-on of his native country; he gave lectures and wrote newspaper articles on Irish topics, and all his published work engages, sometimes critically, sometimes fondly, with the minutiae of Irish culture, geography, history and politics. Even *Finnegans Wake*, at first sight a huge self-contained puzzle, and on further acquaintance a panorama of some kind of universal history, is, on careful examination, deeply concerned with the events in Ireland that shaped the coming into being of the Free State and eventually, after Joyce's death, the Republic. At the same time, he was living on a continent shaken by two world wars – in both of which he was forced to leave his home – and this experience inevitably wove itself into his writing. Of course, the few hundred words from each work discussed in this book cannot possibly stand for the tens of thousands Joyce published; they may, however, provide a starting place from which to explore one of the most influential and, what is more important, enjoyable literary œuvres of the twentieth century.

A word needs to be said about the vast mountain of critical commentary and reference material that has been published on Joyce. Today, even the most assiduous scholar could not hope to read everything that has been written on him; and anyone other than the Joyce scholar can ignore most of it. Fortunately, there are a number of good introductions available, most of which include helpful advice on where to turn for more advanced studies. (See 'Suggestions for Further Reading' in this book for a few places to start.) Many readers approaching Joyce for the first time feel the need to prepare themselves by reading commentaries first, and then turning assiduously to annotations as they work their way through the book. There is a danger in this reliance on secondary materials, since the pleasure of reading Joyce lies partly in making discoveries and tracing connections for oneself. Consulting the commentators will usually reveal yet more allusions and echoes, but this can be left to a later stage of one's engagement with the text.

Beyond the introductions and annotated editions, there are studies of every conceivable aspect of Joyce's writing, and several journals publish articles three or four times a year. There is a vast amount of material on the Web. Joyce's work has proved to be fertile ground for almost every trend in literary criticism and theory that has emerged since he died, including New Criticism, stylistics, feminism, deconstruction, New Historicism, queer theory, post-colonialism, race studies, animal studies, cultural studies, ethical studies and disability studies. Joyce's manuscripts, which are currently the subject of extensive research activity, have provided evidence of his working methods that throw a fascinating light on his writings. In particular, we are acquiring a better understanding of how those methods changed as he laboured on *Ulysses* and were consolidated as he brought *Finnegans Wake* slowly into being. These procedures were unprecedented in the history of literary creation. Joyce assembled large quantities of brief notes – usually just phrases that caught his attention in books, newspapers or conversation – then sorted these into categories and wove them into the skeletal beginnings of chapters. *Finnegans Wake* is a vast compendium or collage of scraps of the culture that surrounded him (including that culture's history and its relations with other cultures), and although we need have no knowledge of the notebooks and drafts in order to read it, awareness of his procedures provides a fuller sense of what it is we are reading.

My own writing on Joyce over twenty-five years has engaged with many of these approaches, but at the heart of my interest has always been Joyce's handling of language. This is a broader topic than it sounds: it includes Joyce's ability to surprise the reader on every page, using words alone to evoke the most intimate human fears and desires, capturing the tiny details of a city's social and political life, and discovering the comedy in the way we interact with our world. It extends to his reinvigoration of the tradition of the novel, his simultaneous exploitation and critique of the conventions of realism, his demonstration of the endless potential of verbal art. And it points towards his ethical engagement with the question of how individuals and groups treat one another and the environments they inhabit. By tracing some of these issues in short excerpts from Joyce's major works I hope to offer a way into reading Joyce that will bring long-lasting rewards to those who turn, with the requisite open-mindedness, to the works themselves.

1

DUBLINERS: A STYLE OF SCRUPULOUS MEANNESS

I went in on tiptoe. The room through the lace end of the blind was suffused with dusky golden light amid which the candles looked like pale thin flames. He had been coffined. Nannie gave the lead and we three knelt down at the foot of the bed. I pretended to pray but I could not gather my thoughts because the old woman's mutterings distracted me. I noticed how clumsily her skirt was hooked at the back and how the heels of her cloth boots were trodden down all to one side. The fancy came to me that the old priest was smiling as he lay there in his coffin.

But no. When we rose and went up to the head of the bed I saw that he was not smiling. There he lay, solemn and copious, vested as for the altar, his large hands loosely retaining a chalice. His face was very truculent, grey and massive, with black cavernous nostrils and circled by a scanty white fur. There was a heavy odour in the room, the flowers.

We blessed ourselves and came away. In the little room downstairs we found Eliza seated in his armchair in state. I groped my way towards my usual chair in the corner while Nannie went to the sideboard and brought out a decanter of sherry and some wineglasses. She set these on the table and invited us to take a little glass of wine. Then, at her sister's bidding, she poured out the sherry into the glasses and passed them to us. She pressed me to take some cream crackers also but I declined because I thought I would make too much noise eating them. She seemed to be somewhat disappointed at my refusal and went over quietly to the sofa where she sat down behind her sister. No-one spoke: we all gazed at the empty fireplace.

My aunt waited until Eliza sighed and then said:

—Ah, well, he's gone to a better world.

Eliza sighed again and bowed her head in assent. My aunt fingered the stem of her wineglass before sipping a little.

—Did he . . . peacefully? she asked.

—O, quite peacefully, ma'am, said Eliza. You couldn't tell when the breath went out of him. He had a beautiful death, God be praised.

'The Sisters', *Dubliners*, pp. 8–9

In the middle of 1904, the Dublin literary lion George Russell, to whom Joyce had shown his poems two years earlier, invited the 22-year-old to contribute a story to *The Irish Homestead*, the weekly magazine of the Irish Agricultural Organisation Society, and in response the young man wrote a very short piece called 'The Sisters'. It was to be his first published fiction. Over the next three years he wrote another fourteen stories to create a collection he called *Dubliners* – although it took a further seven years and repeated rejections before he found a publisher willing to take on a book which depicted sexual situations, used swear words, named real Dublin establishments, and treated Edward VII disrespectfully. By this time Joyce had been living out of Ireland – primarily in Trieste – for ten years, and his second major work, *A Portrait of the Artist as a Young Man*, was appearing in serialized form.

Dubliners is a deceptive work. Compared to Joyce's three later fictional masterpieces, with their teeming pages, it seems at first glance to be insubstantial; Joyce himself described its style as one of 'scrupulous meanness'. The greatest challenge it poses for the reader lies not in any complexity of language or obscurity of allusion but in the apparent sparseness of each of the little narratives. Hardly anything of any great significance seems to happen, and when it does – there are a couple of deaths and an engagement – its role in the story is not that of the conventional climax. To enjoy *Dubliners* fully it is necessary to savour the details as well as the larger narratives, to be alert to slight shifts of style and attitude, and to relish the ever-present possibility of irony.

Understood in the broadest way, the theme of *Dubliners* is a grand one: the moral and political paralysis, as Joyce saw it, of Dublin at the end of the nineteenth century, and by extension the deadening effect on any population of a hypocritical religious institution abetted by a self-serving political class. The malaise that Joyce identified was exacerbated by Ireland's subservient status within the British archipelago, without its own government and ambivalent about its own culture and traditions. But to extract this simple critical point from the stories is to reduce them to mere slogans. When Joyce said he wanted to offer the Irish 'one good look at themselves' in his 'nicely polished looking-glass', he was emphasizing the degree to which he had reflected the minutest nuances of the lives and feelings of his characters, and the larger themes derive their freshness and interest from their emergence out of these tiny facets. This is why the stories are resonant for readers who have no particular interest in the social and political history of Ireland: they trace the urges and disappointments, deceptions and self-deceptions of characters not too different from ourselves and our acquaintances.

Moreover, in developing a style that would do justice to these subtleties, Joyce had to reinvent the short story, and part of the pleasure of reading *Dubliners* is to savour his extraordinarily original deployment of this familiar literary form. Anyone who knows Chekhov's short stories will recognize a possible forebear, although Joyce claimed not to have read them when he wrote what he called his 'chapter in the moral history of my country'. Following the stories sentence by sentence one can feel the familiar patterns used by earlier, and indeed most later, writers being stretched and tested: the introduction of characters, the descriptions of settings, the use of dialogue, the narration of events, are never entirely what one expects. This sense of constant slight surprise is part of the special experience of reading *Dubliners*. Joyce had begun his writing career composing very short 'epiphanies', many of them records of brief and outwardly quite banal events or conversations that seemed to him to carry great spiritual weight, and the stories of *Dubliners* have a similar structure of outward simplicity and inner significance.

In the context of Irish cultural politics, *Dubliners* was a striking rejection of the dominant mode of the turn of the century: the rediscovery and rewriting of ancient Irish folklore and myth, the magical and mysterious world of the Celtic Twilight. To Joyce, the Irish Revival of Douglas Hyde, George Russell, Augusta Gregory, J. M. Synge and Yeats cast a delusive mist over the harsh realities of Irish life for the majority of the island's inhabitants, and indulged in fanciful language when what was called for was precise and economical prose. Joyce's Catholic, middle-class upbringing kept him apart from the ethos of the Revival, which had a strong Protestant, aristocratic bias. Even George Moore, who in *The Untilled Field* (1903) had published short stories about the Irish peasantry that foreshadowed Joyce's use of an unadorned style, was not realist enough. (*The Untilled Field* was written for translation into Irish; Joyce, by contrast, did not know Irish and distanced himself from what he saw as the parochialism of the Irish language movement.) Impressed by Flaubert's obsession with exactness of phrasing and by Ibsen's goal of exposing what middle-class refinement and the political establishment tried to keep hidden, he introduced an alternative model into Irish writing, one that proved profoundly influential for his successors.

Not that the effect was immediate; in fact, *Dubliners* did not make much of a splash when it was finally published in 1914. (Joyce was to complain that his works had a habit of appearing on the brink of world wars.) During the year of its publication it sold 499 copies, one short of the number needed for Joyce to start receiving royalties; in the following six months, only twenty-six copies. There was little attention in the literary reviews – though Pound, later to become one of Joyce's most important supporters, admired the stories' 'clear hard prose'.

The initial three stories of the collection are presented in the first person, the narrator being a young boy (perhaps the same young boy in all three; he is not given a name). 'The Sisters', which opens the collection and is a longer version of the story published in *The Irish Homestead*, concerns the death of a priest, Father Flynn, who had befriended the boy; in this passage, the narrator visits the priest's house with his aunt to view the body and commiserate with the dead man's two sisters, Nannie and Eliza. By means of this oblique approach, Joyce offers a startlingly different view of Catholicism in Ireland from that of traditional fiction on the subject. The last part of the passage is a dialogue between Eliza and the aunt, with direct speech presented in Joyce's preferred manner: an initial dash, and no indication of the end of the utterance. A little confusing at first, it is something readers of Joyce become quickly accustomed to.

One of the fascinating features of the story (like the two other first-person stories in the collection) is the way Joyce succeeds in combining the boy's view of events with hints of how they appear to an adult consciousness. He does this partly by shifts in style. A simple opening sentence that could have been spoken by the boy – 'I went in on tiptoe' – is followed by one that could only be uttered by an adult, and a writer of literature for that matter, someone who uses words like 'suffused' and 'amid'. It is an example of 'fine writing', certainly, but highly successful fine writing, poetic in its varying sounds and rhythm and vivid in bringing before us the candles that, paradoxically, themselves look like flames in the gloom. As this and many other examples indicate, there is no doubt that Joyce could have produced a series of beautifully written, highly evocative, works that would have been a pleasure to read, at least in small doses, but would have had no long-lasting effect either on readers or on twentieth-century literature. (Most of his published poems, in fact, fall into this category.) However, we must not overlook the fact that, although it does not use the boy's vocabulary, the sentence captures with immense precision the visual impact of walking into the laying-out room for someone whose senses are alert and who is not subject to the conventional attitudes to death of adulthood.

A later example of adult language overlaying the boy's simpler style is the description of the priest in his coffin, though here one feels Joyce pushing at the limits of conventional literary prose in conveying the impression being made on the young narrator. 'Copious' is a remarkable term to describe a corpse (with perhaps a hint of a pun on 'cope', a religious vestment); 'retaining' is aptly mechanical in comparison with the more obvious word 'holding'; and 'black cavernous nostrils' has a nightmarish quality about it. (In the first version, Joyce wrote 'distended nostrils', and there is no doubt that the revision increases the awful power of the corpse's face.) Through these images, which echo some of the disturbing features of the boy's memories, we are given a sense of religion's sheer amoral power, beyond its comforting messages of hope and salvation.

Most of the language of the passage, and of the story, however, does not have a literary quality to it, and the reader may feel that it is all too matter-of-fact. Yet it is its plainness that enables it to capture so perfectly the complex feelings of the boy. Look at the sentence about the boy's inability to pray: a perfectly true-to-life statement, hinting at his momentary irritation at 'the old woman's mutterings'. Then, as if in atonement for this feeling of annoyance, a sentence revealing the boy's sharp observation of the evidence of Nannie's hard life and lack of money: her clumsily hooked skirt and her trodden-down heels. The sentence doesn't overtly indicate compassion on the boy's part, but a degree of sympathy is implicit in the detail. We then move from acute observation to sheer fantasy as the boy imagines the old man in the coffin – which he hasn't yet approached – with a smiling face. This veering from observation to imagination is typical of the boys in all the initial stories; in fact, it is typical of Joyce, even in his early epiphanies.

The story's title is intriguing: we are over halfway through before the two sisters, Nannie and Eliza, are mentioned, in the paragraph before the quoted passage. A more logical title would have been 'The Priest', since the first half of the story is taken up with the boy's response to the news of the priest's death and recollections of his visits to him. But in this passage, and the further three pages before the story ends (with Eliza's account of the priest's mental deterioration before he died), we do get an extraordinarily economical picture of the two women, the active, unspeaking Nannie and the sedentary, talkative Eliza. We are left to work out for ourselves the reason for the differences between them. Nannie is the subservient one (she fills the sherry glasses 'at her sister's bidding' and sits 'behind her sister'), her clothing – as we've seen – betraying evidence of poverty and hard work, while Eliza sits in her dead brother's armchair 'in state' and makes appropriate conversation. Although nothing is said directly about Nannie's state of health, it has been made evident by the way Nannie is greeted that she is deaf, and instead of speaking she points upstairs and then beckons the aunt and the boy into the deadroom. It seems likely, then, that when Nannie 'presses' the boy to take cream crackers, she does it by gesture rather than by words. All we hear from her in the story are her 'mutterings'.

Although Eliza's remarks are conventional, she at least is prepared to say what she means; the boy's aunt, by contrast, although (or because) she has higher class pretensions – Eliza calls her 'ma'am' – is entirely at the mercy of a misguided sense of propriety and politeness. She doesn't speak until Eliza's sigh seems to give her permission to do so, and she cannot pronounce the word 'die' or name the events she is asking about. The boy's embarrassment can only be inferred, as Joyce simply records the exchange; but we have earlier seen him declining the cream crackers and we are aware that he is highly self-conscious in this situation. With the minimum of information – since we are told nothing that the boy is not seeing or thinking – we gain a vivid sense of the two women's ways of coping with the difficulties of their existence, of the boy's complex response to them (we might contrast the disapproval of 'in state' with the regret of 'she seemed to be somewhat disappointed'), and of the aunt's thoroughly conformist behaviour.

There are many more details that play a part in the concentrated evocativeness of this passage, and the entire story – the entire collection, in fact – deploys details in a similar way. After the first three, the stories use third-person narrators, in a manner that is never straightforward: they often present the view of one of the characters rather than adopting an evenhanded approach, and in making value judgements the reader needs to be aware that all is not as straightforward as it seems.[6] The collection is also a carefully structured whole. Joyce indicated in a letter to his brother Stanislaus that the stories are ordered into four groups: stories of childhood (actually, he says 'my childhood'), adolescence, mature life and public life. Although he still had three stories to complete when he wrote this letter, the final order he chose makes the grouping clear: (1) childhood: 'The Sisters', 'An Encounter' and 'Araby' – the first-person stories; (2) adolescence (which, for Joyce, clearly lasted beyond the teens): 'Eveline', 'After the Race', 'Two Gallants' and 'The Boarding House'; (3) mature life: 'A Little Cloud', 'Counterparts', 'Clay' and 'A Painful Case'; and (4) public life: 'Ivy Day in the Committee Room', 'A Mother', and 'Grace'. The fifteenth story, 'The Dead', undertaken two years later than the majority of the others, stands somewhat apart, being longer and less severe in tone. Many of the characters from these stories – most of whom belong to the lower fringes of the middle class, constantly struggling to maintain their class position – appear again in *Ulysses*, sometimes revealing changes in their lives, usually for the worse, since the events of the earlier book.

Extrapolating from this passage and this story, one can begin to appreciate the remarkable achievement of *Dubliners*. What appear to be simple stories can be read again and again, with increasing enjoyment as the tensions and ironies become more evident and the tiniest elements take on more and more meaning. Without indulging in moralization or grandstanding, Joyce anatomizes Dublin's religious, political and cultural life. Religion offers consolation to the self-seeking, sex is disfigured and traded, political life is trivialized and venial. Youthful dreams are exposed as empty; fantasies are shown to be necessary self-deceptions. Education, business and culture are in the hands of small-minded men. However, there are occasional flickerings of passion, of resistance, of beauty; and the language in which this imperfect society is portrayed conveys its own sense of the delicacy of perception and the transforming power of verbal creativity. With the most meagre apprenticeship, Joyce had made himself a master of the art of the short story. Yet he was never to write another one.

2

A PORTRAIT OF THE ARTIST AS A YOUNG MAN I: THE CHILD

It pained him that he did not know well what politics meant and that he did not know where the universe ended. He felt small and weak. When would he be like the fellows in poetry and rhetoric? They had big voices and big boots and they studied trigonometry. That was very far away. First came the vacation and then the next term and then vacation again and then again another term and then again the vacation. It was like a train going in and out of tunnels and that was like the noise of the boys eating in the refectory when you opened and closed the flaps of the ears.

* * *

Only prayers in the chapel and then bed. He shivered and yawned. It would be lovely in bed after the sheets got a bit hot. First they were so cold to get into. He shivered to think how cold they were first. But then they got hot and then he could sleep. It was lovely to be tired. He yawned again. Night prayers and then bed: he shivered and wanted to yawn. It would be lovely in a few minutes. He felt a warm glow creeping up from the cold shivering sheets, warmer and warmer till he felt warm all over, ever so warm and yet he shivered a little and still wanted to yawn.

The bell rang for night prayers and he filed out of the

studyhall after the others and down the staircase and along
the corridors to the chapel. The corridors were darkly lit and
the chapel was darkly lit. Soon all would be dark and sleeping.
There was cold night air in the chapel and the marbles were
the colour the sea was at night. The sea was cold day and
night: but it was colder at night. It was cold and dark under
the seawall beside his father's house. But the kettle would be
on the hob to make punch.

A Portrait of the Artist as a Young Man, chapter I, pp. 12–13

Before his first fictional foray into print with 'The Sisters' in
1904, Joyce had begun an ambitious and fairly traditional
autobiographical novel whose protagonist he called Stephen
Daedalus, the name – combining a Christian saint and a
mythical Greek craftsman – he was also to use as a pseudonym
for the publication of his short story. He called the huge novel
Stephen Hero, on the model of 'Turpin Hero', an anonymous
ballad about the famous highwayman he is said to have sung
at parties. In 1905, having completed twenty-four of the
planned sixty-three chapters, he set it aside to concentrate on
Dubliners, and by the time he returned to it his entire con-
ception of the work had changed. First serialized in 1914–15
and then published in the United States as a book in 1916, the
revised novel covered the same territory – the life of an aspir-
ing Dublin writer from childhood to college – but its new
title, *A Portrait of the Artist as a Young Man*, signals, ironically,
the distance from his earlier self which Joyce had achieved.
Whether 'the artist' refers to the actual creator of the work (as
in paintings with similar titles), thus highlighting the autobiographical dimension, or whether it indicates a more generic
notion of artisthood, the final phrase cannot but suggest a
contrast between youth and maturity. But unlike 'The Sisters',
A Portrait avoids intimations in the writing itself of the older
author's presence; the style matches each stage of development

of the subject, and the reader is left to judge the degree of irony with which his attitudes and actions are to be viewed.

Joyce never finished, or published, *Stephen Hero*, though after his death an edition of the surviving fragments – some eleven chapters – was brought out. *A Portrait* marks a radical shift from the earlier project, and constituted a breakthrough (not just for its author but for European literature) in its evocation of a growing boy's developing sense of language and its potential in the world, from the innocent responsiveness of the child to the would-be sophistication of the young adult. In five long chapters Joyce charts his hero's growth not by a continuous narrative but by a series of episodes separated sometimes by extensive temporal gaps. Part of the interest of each one is registering the new phase of Stephen's growth and what it implies about the intervening period; and it is often the details of the language that provide the most subtle clues. And there is much to engage the reader in each phase: we follow Stephen's intense responses to the conflicts of Irish politics, the demands of sexual desire, the temptations of the religious life, the orthodoxies and restrictions of a moralistic society, the passions of friendship and the fascinations of art, all taking place against the background of a family slipping inexorably down the economic ladder, just as Joyce's own family did.

Reactions to the work were mixed: many reviewers admired the vividness of Joyce's representation of a boy's and a young man's psychology, the variety and power of the writing, the honesty of the treatment of sex and religion. Many others found it disgusting in its use of 'privy-language' and its interest in 'the sex-torments of adolescence' (to quote one reviewer); others thought it long-winded and inattentive to the reader's needs. Pound, through whose efforts the novel was first published as a serial in the English little magazine *The Egoist*, promoted it as a truly European work in the tradition of Flaubert. Wells, who admired the novel immensely in spite of his commitment to a very different kind of fiction, was more aware of its Irish, and anti-English, dimension, a dimension that has only fairly recently been fully explored. The variety of responses matched the complexity of the book, which provides a series of images of turn-of-the-century Dublin through eyes growing in acuity and a mind increasing in disenchantment, until complete rejection seems the only solution – yet one that the book's ironies keep the reader from entirely accepting. This Ireland is emphatically not the Ireland of the Irish Revivalists, whose star, in any case, was beginning to fade. In the year the book was first published, the Easter Rising in Dublin marked a turning point in Ireland's history, and the traumatic years that followed had less room for dreams of a mythical past.

Young Stephen Dedalus (Joyce changed the surname from Daedalus, making it slightly less Greek) is a boarder at Clongowes Wood College, the Jesuit-run school in county Kildare that Joyce himself had been sent to at the age of six. It is the year 1891, when Joyce would have been nine; unlike Joyce, however, Stephen – who is also about nine – appears to be in his initial term at school, counting the days to the Christmas vacation when he will return home. The first of the two episodes set at Clongowes follows Stephen from the evening of a day in October to the following evening; within this short span of time, Joyce conveys vividly a young child's experience of strangeness and alienation as he adapts to a new and often harsh environment. The vividness of this particular twenty-four hours is augmented by Stephen's having contracted a fever, although we are not told explicitly of this since he is not aware of the cause of his unnaturally sharp perceptions.

His new surroundings keep exposing his ignorance: at the moment captured in the passage above, he is supposed to be studying his geography lesson but the textbook has instead set off a train of associations leading him to think about political arguments at home and about the extent of the universe. Joyce has created a style that, while not imitating the writing of a boy of Stephen's age (it does not have mistakes, for instance), conveys his unsophisticated thought patterns and elementary grasp of concepts. Much of it is in what is known as 'free indirect discourse': the grammatical form of the sentences is that of ordinary narration (not 'then I can sleep' but 'then he could sleep'), but the vocabulary and style are those of the character. The sentences are simple and short, and Joyce does not avoid the repetitions that would be objectionable in a mature style: 'did not know' – 'did not know'; 'big voices' – 'big boots'.

The repetitions that make up the alternation of term time and vacation are expressed in repetitions in the language, as Stephen counts out to himself the new organizing rhythm of his life. He is no longer trying to solve the riddles of politics or astronomy, nor processing his new life: his feverishness has concentrated his attention on his own body and on his immediate need for sleep and warmth. The ideas of coldness and heat dominate his thoughts as he imagines being in bed. If we pick out the words that signal these ideas we find a chain of terms in which neither state feels permanent, since each gives way eventually to its opposite: 'shivered' – 'hot' – 'cold' – 'shivered' – 'cold' – 'hot' – 'shivered' – 'warm' – 'cold' – 'shivering' – 'warmer' – 'warmer' – 'warm' – 'warm' – 'shivered'. What comes across are not just ideas, of course, but that physical experience of sensitivity to both warmth and cold that we associate with a heightened body temperature; particularly telling is the displacement of the boy's own state to the 'cold shivering sheets' he imagines touching his skin. Stephen does not know it, but his shivering and yawning (and, in an example of Joyce's accuracy as a recorder of physical experience, *wanting* to yawn without being able to do so) are symptoms of an incipient fever that will cause him to be sent to the sickroom the following morning, symptoms which the reader has noticed from much earlier in this episode.

Repetition, therefore, serves Joyce's purposes as a realistic evocation of a child's way of thinking and, at the same time, as a particularly effective way of conveying powerful experiences, physical and psychological, to the reader. Writers who look back at childhood experience in adult language can often diminish its intensity by framing it in a mature outlook. There is a degree of such framing in 'The Sisters', though the adult language in that case serves as a substitute for the boy's intensity of feeling. Here, however, Joyce conveys Stephen's experience, and Stephen's language, to us without modification.

Not only the syntax but the vocabulary, too, is appropriate for a child. Most of the words are simple, and the adjectives in particular lack the detail of an older speaker: 'small', 'weak', 'big', 'hot', 'cold', 'lovely', 'warm', and so on. However, one occasionally senses that Stephen's use of a word is in part an attempt to explore its meaning for himself. He has been doing this with 'politics' and 'universe' and now he is getting to grips with the words, and concepts, 'vacation' and 'term', further extending an analogy that had come to him earlier in the evening when, in a spasm of misery in the refectory, he had 'leaned his elbows on the table and shut and opened the flaps of his ears' (p. 9). But there is one word Stephen clearly does not know the meaning of – and it is his ignorance that is significant. The older boys – always a source of particular fascination and fear for the younger boys – not only have big voices and big boots but they study something called 'trigonometry'. Stephen has no doubt heard this impressive-sounding word, and for him it stands for that world of learning from which he is excluded and to which, at this stage of his life, he cannot imagine gaining access.

The bell rings and the pupils leave the studyhall, Stephen apparently bringing up the rear. (Notice how Joyce omits the hyphen when he writes 'studyhall'; this will become a trademark of his style, often producing a more concentrated compound word than the normal hyphenated version.) Again we are given only Stephen's perceptions, and only in language appropriate to his age and his physical condition. Repetition is once more a feature of the prose, and once more the words are simple ones: 'darkly lit', 'darkly lit', 'dark', 'dark'; 'cold', 'cold', 'colder', 'cold'; 'night', 'night', 'night', 'night'. As he sits in the chapel for prayers, he is aware of little other than the coldness and the darkness, both of which seem concentrated in the marble chapel furnishings, which are 'the colour the sea was at night'. It is at once a childish association in childishly laborious language (not 'the colour of the sea at night') and a striking one. The experience producing the association is less one of colour – the sea at night is black or very close to it, as no doubt are the marbles – than one of being enclosed by a cold substance: Stephen moves from the 'cold night air' to the marbles to the night sea, and then in the following sentence to the coldness of the sea. Here is a similar process of puzzling something out for himself that he had been through with regard to politics, the universe, and the rhythm of term and vacation. It is a process that characterizes much of Stephen's intellectual growth from the first page of the book, where we encounter the beginnings of his observations about the changing temperatures in bed: 'When you wet the bed first it is warm then it gets cold.'

The reason why Stephen's thoughts swerve to the sea when there is no apparent cause becomes clearer in the penultimate sentence: the sea is associated with his home, just as the train which provides him with an analogy for the term–vacation rhythm is in his mind because it is what will take him back to his family for Christmas. And the warmth and security of home is felt all the more strongly when it is imagined in con-trast to the cold and dark outside – and, more specifically, to the seawall holding back the accumulation of cold and dark-ness in those black waters. The vocabulary suddenly changes as a comforting image comes to Stephen's mind: the cheerful kettle next to the fire in readiness for a warming drink.

The brilliance of Joyce's writing is such that the subtlety of his method is scarcely noticed by most readers, who respond directly to its evocation of childhood intensities of emotion and physical experience. Although in his later works there is often a more showy aspect to his stylistic achievements, the sure touch he exhibits in choosing the right word for the purpose seldom abandoned him.

3

A PORTRAIT OF THE ARTIST AS A YOUNG MAN II: THE ARTIST

He drew forth a phrase from his treasure and spoke it softly to himself:—A day of dappled seaborne clouds.

The phrase and the day and the scene harmonised in a chord. Words. Was it their colours? He allowed them to glow and fade, hue after hue: sunrise gold, the russet and green of apple orchards, azure of waves, the greyfringed fleece of clouds. No, it was not their colours: it was the poise and balance of the period itself. Did he then love the rhythmic rise and fall of words better than their associations of legend and colour? Or was it that, being as weak of sight as he was shy of mind, he drew less pleasure from the reflection of the glowing sensible world through the prism of a language manycoloured and richly storied than from the contemplation of an inner world of individual emotions mirrored perfectly in a lucid supple periodic prose?

He passed from the trembling bridge on to firm land again. At that instant, as it seemed to him, the air was chilled; and looking askance towards the water he saw a flying squall darkening and crisping suddenly the tide. A faint click at his heart, a faint throb in his throat told him once more of how his flesh dreaded the cold infrahuman odour of the sea: yet he did not strike across the downs on his left but held straight on along the spine of rocks that pointed against the river's mouth.

* * *

In the distance along the course of the slowflowing Liffey slender masts flecked the sky and, more distant still, the dim fabric of the city lay prone in haze. Like a scene on some vague arras, old as man's weariness, the image of the seventh city of christendom was visible to him across the timeless air, no older nor more weary nor less patient of subjection than in the days of the thingmote.

Disheartened, he raised his eyes towards the slowdrifting clouds, dappled and seaborne. They were voyaging across the deserts of the sky, a host of nomads on the march, voyaging high over Ireland, westward bound. The Europe they had come from lay out there beyond the Irish Sea, Europe of strange tongues and valleyed and woodbegirt and citadelled and of entrenched and marshalled races. He heard a confused music within him as of memories and names which he was almost conscious of but could not capture even for an instant; then the music seemed to recede, to recede, to recede: and from each receding trail of nebulous music there fell always one longdrawn calling note, piercing like a star the dusk of silence. Again! Again! Again! Again! A voice from beyond the world was calling.

—Hello, Stephanos!

—Here comes The Dedalus!

—Ao! . . . Eh, give it over, Dwyer, I'm telling you or I'll give you a stuff in the kisser for yourself . . . Ao!

A Portrait of the Artist as a Young Man, chapter IV, pp. 160–61

Young Stephen is obliged to leave Clongowes, as his real-life model had to do, when the family fortunes decline, and after a spell at home (or rather homes, since the financial difficulties entail several decampings) he is enrolled at Belvedere College, another Jesuit school, this time in the centre of Dublin. (Again, he is following in Joyce's own footsteps.)

While he is there, a three-day religious retreat for the pupils has a profound effect on him: in an act of confession he admits that he has been seeking sex with prostitutes and, feeling cleansed, he embraces a new devotional regimen. His evident religious commitment leads to an interview with the director of the school, who proposes that he train for the priesthood. It is a decision on which the entire course of his life will depend. As he imagines his first night in the dormitory as a novice, memories of the cold corridors of Clongowes flood back; there is an echo of the earlier passage as he feels 'a feverish quickening of the pulses'; and he realizes that he cannot go down this road.

Casting off his adolescent piety, he experiences a new attachment to his family, in all their neediness, and a new possibility presents itself thanks to his academic achievements: the university. (Not Trinity College, a Protestant stronghold at the time, but University College, Dublin, then under Jesuit auspices.) While his father is discussing this possibility with the Belvedere tutor, Stephen, impatient at the long wait, heads towards the nearby Bull, the seawall that forms one of the arms containing Dublin Bay. It is a moment at which an alternative pathway is opening up for him, central to which will be the art of the writer.

Jumping to the passage above – it comes towards the end of the fourth chapter – from the one discussed previously makes the shift in style obvious. Once again Joyce uses free indirect discourse, so that what appears to be a narrator's description is coloured by the kind of vocabulary and syntax Stephen himself might use at this stage of his life. He is now perhaps sixteen years old, and has absorbed the language and some of the attitudes of his favourite poets. The nineteenth century is almost at its end, and many of the highly regarded writers of the day value fine expression over strict realism. We can see their influence on Stephen not only in the phrase he utters in response to the scene before him – 'A day of dappled seaborne clouds' – but in the language by means of which the action is described. 'He drew forth a phrase from his treasure' is just a little too precious to be taken entirely seriously: Stephen's image of his mind as a trove of poetic expressions suggests that he has some way to go before he will achieve maturity as an artist.

At the same time, Stephen's fascination with language, which has been a continuous thread from the beginning of the book, holds some promise for the budding writer. He doesn't simply take for granted the poetic quality of the phrase he has spoken to himself; he interrogates its power to charm and move him. In so doing, he explores two possible sources of this power: the play of images conjured up by the words, and their shapeliness of sound and rhythm – what he calls 'the poise and balance of the period itself'. Before rejecting the former, he gives it its full due by dwelling on the colours suggested by each significant word, *day, dappled, seaborne, clouds.* However, this elaboration can itself only be carried out in further words, which both strengthens and weakens Stephen's argument against the power of images – strengthens it, because it shows that we never escape the words into a realm of pure colour, weakens it, because these further phrases do succeed in evoking a rich sense of the different colours. (Note again two of Joyce's fused compounds, 'seaborne' and 'greyfringed'; there are many other examples in the passage.)

The preference that he exhibits for the sound and movement of the words over their semantic associations could lead to writing of superficial beauty but little strength – a failing to which Joyce was not immune, particularly in his poetry, though he succumbed to a lesser extent than many of his contemporaries. The phrase he is investigating is not without semantic interest, but Stephen ignores this aspect: in particular, we might ask, how can clouds be said to be 'seaborne'? It requires an annotated edition to discover that the phrase is not original to Stephen, but in the book he has taken it from the adjective is the more logical 'breeze-borne'.[7] Yet 'seaborne' has a resonant suggestiveness that the more obvious alternative lacks, inviting us to puzzle over it a moment: are the clouds being borne across the sea? or are they borne by (and born from) the sea's moisture?

It is also to Stephen's credit that he is willing to entertain a somewhat reductive explanation for his predilection: his shortsightedness, which may be what leads him to prefer language's evocation of the inner realm of feeling over its representation of shapes and colours. Yet the passage demonstrates that these are not separable: Stephen's feelings are conveyed as much by the words detailing what he sees as those dealing directly with his inner experience. Take the second sentence of the following paragraph: he senses a sudden coldness in the air, and looking towards the water sees 'a flying squall darkening and crisping suddenly the tide'. It is a wonderfully economic description, each word contributing fully to the mobile image, the slightly unusual placing of the adverb adding urgency to the motion, the verb 'crisping' retaining its older meaning of 'curling' with an added suggestion of 'making chilly' (as in a 'crisp morning'). But at the same time, the sudden change in the sea's appearance (occurring, so it seems to Stephen, at the moment he steps onto firm land) implies a change in his outlook, as the word 'askance' also suggests. This is confirmed by the surprising 'faint click at his heart' and 'faint throb in his throat' that accompany his registering of the alteration in the weather; now it becomes difficult to separate the inner and outer worlds, as Stephen seems to hear and feel his own bodily organs. These bare monosyllables convey admirably the tug of fear that is as much physical as emotional, and we note too that it is his 'flesh' that dreads the sea's odour, as if his entire body were possessed of the sense of smell. We recall young Stephen at Clongowes connecting the coldness of the marbles in the dark chapel with the cold, dark sea (and when we meet him again in *Ulysses* his dread of the sea has not abated).

Can we take this compelling writing to be a reflection of Stephen's own skill with words? Is it, that is to say, a form of free indirect discourse, as the previous paragraph clearly is? The question is not easy to answer, and it is one of the fascinating features of the book that we're often not quite sure when we are reading the words of an accomplished storyteller, the narrator created by Joyce, and when we are getting a hint of Stephen's own verbal talents at a particular stage of his life. Here, though, the contrast between the lavish poetic style of the previous paragraph and the vivid economy of this one may suggest that we are now observing Stephen from the outside.

In spite of his feeling of apprehension, Stephen chooses to walk along the wall jutting into the sea (which is made to seem more risky than it really is by the words 'spine', 'rocks' and 'pointing'), rather than the safe ground of North Bull Island to his left. (It is typical of Joyce that this scene of inner drama takes place in a concretely located environment, still traceable in Dublin today; his very distance from Ireland seems to have provoked an obsession with accuracy of geographical detail.) Again the outward action is inseparable from the mental and emotional decision which Stephen is facing: although walking one way rather than another is a trivial choice, and although it is a difficult one only because of an irrational phobia, it signals a will to face danger rather than take the easy option.

The light changes again, as if the threat has been overcome, though not to sunlit brilliance. Instead, all is dim, hazy and vague as Stephen looks across the bay to the city. We are back with the heightened poetic language with which the passage began: words seem chosen for their suggestiveness and emotional effect rather than their visual accuracy. Stephen thinks of the River Liffey as 'slowmoving', though he cannot see its motion from where he is standing; Dublin is lying 'prone' because it seems to him like a lifeless face-down body, though it is hard to give this any literal meaning. Just as the hazy light evens out the visual field, so Stephen's mood banishes any sense that the passage of history brings about change, and consequently any hope of making a difference to the city he has grown up in. His knowledge of history and early literature – evident in his association of the cityscape with the tapestry image on an arras, his allusion to the 'thingmote' or Viking ruling council, and his naming Dublin 'the seventh city of christendom'[8] – produces only a feeling that the centuries have achieved nothing. No wonder he is 'disheartened'.

If Ireland seems to offer no future for the aspirant artist, is there an alternative? Suddenly the narrator's – and presumably Stephen's – language changes gear, as the clouds referred to earlier are transformed into desert travellers and their imagined origin is described in high poetic terms. Europe, strange and romantic, now beckons the would-be artist (for Stephen, 'Europe' clearly means 'continental Europe'); all he has read and heard about crystallizes into a longing to experience the magical centres of the culture that has formed part of his education from childhood. From now to the end of the book these voices call out to Stephen.

But a question haunts the attentive reader. How seriously are we to take Stephen's weary view of his home city and the marvellous European alternative he imagines? Don't those poetic phrases border at times on cliché? 'Old as man's weariness'; 'a host of nomads on the march'; 'woodbegirt and citadelled' – there is a linguistic self-indulgence about such phrases, very different from the sharp economy of 'darkening and crisping suddenly the tide'. And what about the repetition of words? In the earlier episode young Stephen's thoughts are marked by the repetition of key terms, suggesting the stage of linguistic development he has reached; now, however, repetition is a deliberate poetic device which can be powerful but can easily tip into archness or banality. (Where the younger Stephen looks forward to feeling straightforwardly 'tired', it is typical of the older Stephen that the word that comes to mind is the poetic 'weary'.) It is not always easy to say where the borderline lies. For most of this passage, the repetitions seems purposeful and restrained; for instance, 'old' – 'older' and 'weariness' – 'weary' are part of a controlled rhetorical structure, even though the sentiments may not stand up to much scrutiny. But 'music' – 'music' – 'recede' – 'recede' – 'recede' – 'receding' – 'music'? This sequence is harder to justify. Is Stephen allowing himself to fall under the spell of words and their attendant myths? Is there something just a little *too* poetic about the 'one long-drawn calling note, piercing like a star the dusk of silence', attractive though that last complex metaphor is?

One kind of answer is given by Joyce's next novel, *Ulysses*, in which we meet Stephen after his European dream has proved fruitless. But another kind of answer is immediately forthcoming: just as Stephen hears, or imagines he hears, a voice from beyond the world calling to him, another voice breaks in, a voice very much from this world. His school friends are bathing nearby, and their shouts puncture the mood of high poetry. Nothing could be further removed from the language of Stephen's reverie than the coarse repartee of the bantering adolescents. If Stephen wants to succeed as an artist, he has to find a way – as Joyce did – of incorporating these voices as well.

Stephen, however, has yet to see this, and he refuses to join in the horseplay, finding instead his ideal of beauty, and his promise of a new life, in a wading girl. Joyce brings to bear on the scene the full force of his poetic rhetoric, and unless we remember the caustic voices of his schoolmates we are in danger of succumbing to Stephen's vision of himself and his future as an artist. At the same time, it would be wrong to regard such moments as purely ironic: this is indeed a turning point in Stephen's education as an artist, and although he has much more to learn than he realizes, it marks his permanent rejection of the religious life, the other possible vocation that had beckoned.

The final chapter finds Stephen at university, interacting vigorously with fellow students, writing poetry overloaded with vague imagery, pursuing his studies in a less than studious manner, articulating an aesthetic theory, pursuing a frustrating and unsatisfactory involvement with a girl, and feeling more and more the need to escape the confining bounds of home, nation and church. The last few pages, in the form of a diary, give us Stephen's own words as he prepares to leave Ireland, and contain notable signs of a growing maturity in the writing. Not only are some of the entries powerfully evocative without the striving for effect characteristic of his earlier moments of rapture or gloom, but he is now capable of mocking his own excesses. After a highly wrought passage recalling the view of Dublin from the Bull wall – 'Faintly, under the heavy night, through the silence of the city which has turned from dreams to dreamless sleep as a weary lover whom no caresses move . . .' – we find the entry: '*11 April:* Read what I wrote last night. Vague words for a vague emotion' (p. 243). When we meet Stephen again, such self-criticism has become habitual, though the poetic impulse has not been extinguished.

4

ULYSSES I: STEPHEN DEDALUS

Under the upswelling tide he saw the writhing weeds lift languidly and sway reluctant arms, hising up their petticoats, in whispering water swaying and upturning coy silver fronds. Day by day: night by night: lifted, flooded and let fall. Lord, they are weary: and, whispered to, they sigh. Saint Ambrose heard it, sigh of leaves and waves, waiting, awaiting the fullness of their times, *diebus ac noctibus iniurias patiens ingemiscit*. To no end gathered: vainly then released, forthflowing, wending back: loom of the moon. Weary too in sight of lovers, lascivious men, a naked woman shining in her courts, she draws a toil of waters.

Five fathoms out there. Full fathom five thy father lies. At one, he said. Found drowned. High water at Dublin bar. Driving before it a loose drift of rubble, fanshoals of fishes, silly shells. A corpse rising saltwhite from the undertow, bobbing a pace a pace a porpoise landward. There he is. Hook it quick. Pull. Sunk though he be beneath the watery floor.

Ulysses, 3.461–74

To read *Ulysses*, it is not necessary to have read *A Portrait*, but if you have done so, the first three chapters take on an additional layer of meaning. They focus on Stephen Dedalus, clearly the same character who at the end of *A Portrait* was making his preparations to leave Ireland for the Continent. He is now back in Dublin, living in a tower originally built to the south of the city as part of the defences against a possible Napoleonic invasion, together with a medical student named Malachi ('Buck') Mulligan. We gradually learn that the escape to a new world of romantic inspiration that seemed to be the climax just beyond the end of the earlier book was a failure, strengthening in retrospect the irony surrounding Stephen's high-flown ambitions. After only a short stay in Paris, he has returned in response to a telegram from his father with news of his mother's fatal illness, and *Ulysses* opens not long after her death, now a painful memory. He has a job teaching in a school for young boys, an occupation for which he seems sin-gularly unsuited and which he is on the point of resigning from. Although caustic about his own previous efforts as an artist, he has not given up his ambition to write. Much of this, like *A Portrait*, is autobiographical.

These first three episodes constitute what Joyce named in correspondence the 'Telemachia', so-called because Stephen is the modern avatar of Telemachus, Odysseus' son, who, at the start of the *Odyssey*, has heard no news of his father since the fall of Troy ten years earlier. (Although Stephen's father is not missing, he is not making a particularly good job of his pater-nal responsibilities after his wife's death.) Readers new to *Ulysses* are often puzzled by the disparity between its title, implying a rewriting of Homer's epic (using the Latin form of the hero's name), and the absence of section or chapter titles to signal how this relationship operates. To deepen the puzzle, commentators on the work freely refer to the chapters by names taken from episodes or characters in the *Odyssey*, like 'Proteus' or 'Penelope'. These names have not been made up by critics: they were carefully set out by Joyce in a plan of the novel (known as the 'schema') given to friends, but when the book was published he decided to leave them out. Keeping them in mind unquestionably aids the reader in identifying the parallels with the *Odyssey*, but Joyce's omission of them is a useful reminder that these parallels, though they can be part of the fun to be gained from the book, are by no means the only way to enjoy it. *Ulysses* is many things at once, and one of these is a twentieth-century epic that replaces tales of a battle against a giant with a biscuit tin hurled by a bigoted nationalist and enchantment by a sorceress with confrontation by a brothel-keeper – at once implying that our daily adventures are no less important than the heroic deeds of ancient legend, and that ancient legend (the staple of the Irish Revival) had its absurd side too. In choosing as model and butt one of the two great narratives that stand at the origins of Western literature, Joyce made his ambition clear: he would be a Homer for the modern age, substituting comic prose for epic verse and urban contretemps for heroic exploits.

The first three episodes, as they are named in the unpublished plan, are: 'Telemachus', in which we see Stephen's growing animosity towards Buck Mulligan, partly due to the latter's willingness to prostitute himself – and his Irish culture – to a visiting Englishman; 'Nestor', in which Stephen attempts to control his restive class, then receives his pay (and would-be fatherly advice based on ignorance and prejudice) from the school's headmaster; and 'Proteus', in which a stroll on the beach allows Stephen to range widely in thought about, among other things, the past (his and Dublin's), his present situation and his aspirations as a writer. In the *Odyssey*, Nestor is an elderly Greek warrior whom Telemachus consults about his father's whereabouts, and Proteus is the shape-shifting old man of the sea. We can roughly estimate when the chapters are set from their content, but again our task is simplified if we have the information Joyce provided in his schema: they take place at 8 a.m., 10 a.m. and 11 a.m. (It is not until later in the book that we discover the date: Thursday, 16 June 1904 – the year in which Joyce met, and left Ireland with, Nora Barnacle, the woman with whom he was to spend the rest of his life.)

In these chapters, Joyce allows us to eavesdrop on Stephen's thoughts by means of a technique that became known as 'interior monologue', a more direct way of representing the inner world than the free indirect discourse that formed the staple of his earlier works. Although there are some minor precedents for this technique, and Joyce credited its invention to the French novelist Édouard Dujardin in his 1888 work *Les Lauriers sont coupés*, no one had exploited it so extensively or subtly. In the first two chapters, bursts of interior monologue interrupt the third-person, past-tense narrative. It is recognizable both by its content and its form – it is in the first person and the present tense, and its syntax is frequently fragmentary. (There is a hint of what is to come in the passage we looked at in chapter 3: a single-word sentence, 'Words', which we read as something crossing Stephen's mind rather than anything the narrator is saying.) In 'Proteus', however, Stephen's thoughts take centre stage, and the narrator's account of the few actions that occur is reduced to a minimum.

Readers often find these chapters – and in particular the third – a challenge on account of this unfamiliar style, and because Stephen's mind (as we have begun to see in *A Portrait*) is characterized by its store of arcane knowledge and its intellectual bent. Many readers have reached 'Proteus' and then given up. A strategy that can make one's entry into the novel less of a challenge is to start one's reading not with chapter 1 but with chapter 4, which takes place at the same time as chapter 1, but in a different part of Dublin. The advantage of doing this is that the character we meet in chapter 4, Leopold Bloom, has a mind that is much more immediately accessible: like Stephen's, it is filled with a mass of cultural materials, but they tend to be the mental bric-a-brac of a man of unusual curiosity who has read a certain amount of popular science and history, but who does not have Stephen's intellectual and poetic sensibility, nor his familiarity with the further reaches of European high culture. Joyce uses the same interior monologue technique, though of course Bloom has a different style of thought, and the reader quickly becomes adept at reading it. It is possible to read on to chapter 6 before returning to the beginning, since 1–3 and 4–6 occur in parallel, 1 and 4 both taking place at 8 a.m., 2 and 5 at 10 a.m., and 3 and 6 at 11 a.m., with only one moment of direct contact when Bloom sees Stephen from a carriage in chapter 6, the 'Hades' episode. From chapter 7 on, the time sequence is single.

The passage above begins with a sentence that has much in common with the account of Stephen's view of Dublin across the bay in *A Portrait*. Again Stephen is looking at the sea, and again the description has a poetic lavishness about it that suggests a style less the narrator's than Stephen's own. Neologism ('upswelling'), personification ('arms', 'whispering'), alliteration ('writhing weeds . . . lift languidly . . . whispering water'), and repetition ('sway . . . swaying') are effective means of heightening the evocative power of the language, and the image of the moving seaweed is brought vividly before us. But there is an interloper in this verbal splendour: 'hising up their petticoats'. You won't find the verb to 'hise' in the Oxford English Dictionary; it is presumably slang that has never made it into the lexicographer's ken, though it is easy to guess at its meaning. And 'petticoats' seems a little mundane for the immediate context – though it does go with 'reluctant' and 'coy' to associate the seaweed with provocative female sexuality.

The answer to this puzzle points to one of the striking features of *Ulysses*, and one the reader learns to appreciate as

the book goes on. Thirty pages earlier, Stephen had heard a
snatch of bawdy song from Mulligan's lips: '*For old Mary
Ann/She doesn't care a damn./But, hising up her petticoats . . .*'
(1.382–4)[9]. A single phrase thus serves to remind us of the
earlier encounter between Stephen and Mulligan, and adds a
touch of humour to the rather solemn descriptive language. It
suggests that Stephen is still brooding on the exchanges with
his companion (he has decided that he will not go back to the
tower that night), with the further implication that the lyrical
description that surrounds the phrase is all Stephen's. As the
book progresses, however, we find that such recalls of earlier
phrasing do not necessarily indicate a character's memory: it is
as if *Ulysses* has a memory of its own, and part of the pleasure
in reading it is recognizing the repeated, and often comically
transformed, fragments.

What if the reader doesn't recall the earlier passage? This
hardly matters in such a rich text. The amount of detail on
every page of Joyce's last two works means that some is bound
to be missed; however, this is far less important than in most
works of literature, since one is not so much reading *through*
the words to an imagined reality as reading the words themselves as they create, but also sometimes deform or disguise,
that imagined world. To miss a cross-reference or an allusion
is to be deprived of a possible moment of enjoyable connect-
edness, but it is unlikely to result in a misunderstanding of the
plot or misjudgement of the characters.

The paragraph continues in a rhythmic imitation of the to-
and-fro movement of the seaweed, an endless motion which
seems partly to encapsulate and partly to produce Stephen's
mood of world-weariness, reminiscent of his mood in the
passage from *A Portrait*. Typically for Stephen, he finds within
his trove of accumulated learning an ancient counterpart:
Saint Ambrose, commenting on a Biblical passage, describes
the patient earth groaning by day and by night over wrongs.

Most readers face a choice at this point: to turn to an annotation, the Internet or a pile of reference books in order to find a translation, or to read on, aware only that Stephen is connecting his present mood to that of some Church Father who wrote in Latin. On a first-time reading, the second is probably the better choice: part of the point is to appreciate Stephen's mental habits, for which it is not necessary to follow his every intellectual journey, and the full interpretation can wait for later readings.

In the final sentence of this paragraph, Stephen's literary style reaches an extravagance that is hard not to read as parody. The moon – already figured as a loom – is now a naked woman weary at the sight of her lovers; her tidal action seems implied in the final phrase, though its precise meaning remains unclear. (Does 'toil' mean 'net' or 'struggle'? In what sense does she 'draw' it?) Commentators have suggested that there must be a literary allusion here, which seems likely, but nothing that carries conviction has been proposed. New readers of Joyce are sometimes surprised that decades of scholarly activity by an army of critics have still left parts of Joyce's work in obscurity (something that is even truer of *Finnegans Wake*), but they should take heart: the conclusion to be drawn is not that Joyce wrote impossibly difficult books but that there are obscurities that may be left obscure without detracting from understanding and enjoyment.

Having reached this point in the book, the reader can recognize interior monologue instantly, and the next paragraph opens with a clear shift to this mode: 'Five fathoms out there.' Whereas the previous paragraph gave us a kind of idealized version of Stephen's thought processes – what he might write if he were to transcribe his mood onto paper – this one begins with a sentence fragment and a deictic ('there' – a word whose meaning depends on the position in time and space of the speaker or, here, thinker) that we read as actual thought.

(Of course, Joyce is not trying to record exactly what goes on in people's minds; like all literary devices, this is a convention, but one that works with remarkable immediacy.) In this case, not just thought but verbal memory: if we have read so far with attentiveness, we will recall that in the first episode Stephen overheard a boatman using exactly these words as he looked over Dublin Bay. The boatman was commenting on a drowned corpse that, he had asserted, would be swept in with the incoming tide at about one o'clock (1.673–4).

Again Stephen's mind moves to a literary allusion, a more familiar one this time, Ariel's song to Ferdinand in *The Tempest*, a song whose appropriateness for a Telemachus figure – a young man in search of his father – is obvious. After another recollection of the boatman's words and a couple of phrases – 'Found drowned. High water at Dublin bar.' – that echo police reports or inquest findings (the first phrase is also the title of a popular painting in High Victorian style by G. F. Watts), something closer to the poetic mode returns. However, Stephen's language as he imagines the corpse being swept in by the tide is more concrete and vivid than his effusions about the moon. (We may recall the difference between his awareness of the squall and his musings on the city in *A Portrait*.) The forceful description gives way to what seems to be an echo of a nursery rhyme, 'a pace a pace a porpoise', though no commentator has tracked it down, followed some more brief thoughts – Stephen is now imagining the corpse being pulled in – and a further well-known and equally apt quotation, this time from Milton's *Lycidas*. On this occasion the quotation has an additional motivation: Stephen is actually recalling a pupil's unsteady reading of the poem an hour earlier.

Stephen's fear of the sea – and his dislike of water in general – has been a continuous thread from the early pages of *A Portrait*. Here it is combined with the disturbing image of the corpse, which Stephen, and the narrator, describe in vivid detail (we have only the start of the description in the quoted passage). At other times, Stephen's aversion to water, which includes water to wash himself, is a source of comedy, especially in contrast to the figure who comes to supplant him as the imaginative and moral centre of the book, Joyce's modern Odysseus, the thirty-eight-year old Leopold Bloom. Bloom's attraction to water – we are soon to discover him looking forward to a warm bath – is only one of a series of contrasts that will emerge between the two main characters, placing the youthful intensities that have so far dominated the novel into a new, more rounded, perspective.

5

ULYSSES II: LEOPOLD BLOOM

I was happier then. Or was that I? Or am I now I? Twentyeight I was. She twentythree. When we left Lombard street west something changed. Could never like it again after Rudy. Can't bring back time. Like holding water in your hand. Would you go back to then? Just beginning then. Would you? Are you not happy in your home you poor little naughty boy? Wants to sew on buttons for me. I must answer. Write it in the library.

Grafton street gay with housed awnings lured his senses. Muslin prints, silkdames and dowagers, jingle of harnesses, hoofthuds lowringing in the baking causeway. Thick feet that woman has in the white stockings. Hope the rain mucks them up on her. Countrybred chawbacon. All the beef to the heels were in. Always gives a woman clumsy feet. Molly looks out of plumb.

He passed, dallying, the windows of Brown Thomas, silk mercers. Cascades of ribbons. Flimsy China silks. A tilted urn poured from its mouth a flood of bloodhued poplin: lustrous blood. The huguenots brought that here. *Lacaus esant tara tara*. Great chorus that. *Taree tara*. Must be washed in rainwater. Meyerbeer. *Tara: bom bom bom*.

Pincushions. I'm a long time threatening to buy one. Sticking them all over the place. Needles in window curtains.

* * *

Gleaming silks, petticoats on slim brass rails, rays of flat silk stockings.

Useless to go back. Had to be. Tell me all.

Ulysses, 8.608–26, 631–3

During the same period when Stephen is quarrelling with Mulligan, teaching his class and walking on Sandymount Strand, Leopold Bloom, too, is starting his Dublin day. In chapter 4, we see him making a trip to a nearby pork butcher for a breakfast kidney (his Jewishness, while an important aspect of his character and his Dublin existence, doesn't extend to dietary prohibitions), taking his wife Molly her breakfast in bed, learning from her that a concert promoter – one 'Blazes' Boylan – will be visiting her that afternoon, and easing his bowels in the outdoor toilet. (In his unpublished schema, Joyce named the chapter 'Calypso' after the nymph who kept Odysseus in sexual captivity for seven years; Bloom's servitude to Molly is not on quite the same scale, though he clearly appreciates her sensuous physicality.) Chapter 5, which Joyce named 'Lotus-Eaters' after the episode in which some of Odysseus' companions succumb to the lethargy-inducing lotus plant, finds Bloom at a post office some distance away from his Eccles Street home, picking up a letter addressed to him (under the pseudonym 'Henry Flower') and enjoying its mildly salacious contents, encountering an acquaintance who mistakenly believes Bloom is giving him a tip for the Ascot Gold Cup that afternoon, and heading for the 'womb of warmth' offered by the Turkish Baths, where he thinks of masturbating (no doubt over the letter he has received from his female pen pal). Where Odysseus had descended to the land of the dead, Bloom attends a funeral in chapter 6 – hence the title 'Hades' – and for the first time we observe his some-what strained relations with his peers in Dublin society.

Throughout these chapters, we are given Bloom's thoughts in interior monologue, an abundant medley of speculations and fantasies, memories and desires, and responses to sights and smells, which provides a full picture of a modern hero to contrast with Homer's: decidedly unheroic, concerned with the mundane realities of daily life but also blessed with a hugely entertaining capacity to turn them into sources of energetic, if often erratic, mental enquiry.

Thus what looked like being another book about Stephen Dedalus turns out to be much more focused on a character of a completely different kind. Joyce, now in his thirties, living in cosmopolitan Trieste (with a vigorous Jewish community), can no longer identify with the intense young man whose trajectory had been so close to his own. (Though, as we have already seen, by the time he converted *Stephen Hero* into *A Portrait*, that identification was beginning to wear thin.) Stephen's view of art has come to seem too narrow; Joyce now values a greater openness to the variety and unpredictability of experience, a fuller engagement with the worldliness of things, and a personality out of which he can make comedy free of bitterness. But Bloom, although he is said by a fellow Dubliner to have a touch of the artist about him, is no writer; his greatest ambition is to write a story for *Titbits*, the magazine he reads in the outside lavatory – and even that is beyond him. Stephen, we must hope, will learn to move beyond his overblown poetry and his sparse short stories to a new, encyclopaedic, comic mode, as his creator did. At its most vivid and perceptive, his interior monologue suggests a capacity for verbal inventiveness that goes well beyond his literary endeavours, and provides a complement to Bloom's erratic speculations. After these two sequences of three chapters, the clock moves on to noon. Chapter 7, the 'Aeolus' episode, is the first in which the two main characters are to be found in the same place, though without making contact: a newspaper office – a site of windy rhetoric, as the title's reference to the god of the winds suggests. Stephen is trying to make his mark on Dublin's journalistic scene – he tells a short story that meets with little comprehension (in the apparent triviality of its content it is much closer to *Dubliners* than to his somewhat vapid verse) – while Bloom, whose occupation is that of a canvasser for newspaper ads, is on the track of a possible client. It is also the first chapter in which Joyce introduces a stylistic device that moves us completely out of the realm of realism: the whole episode is divided into small sections by imitation newspaper headlines. The source of these headlines is outside the narrative; not for the last time, the text of *Ulysses* exhibits a life, and a creative energy, of its own.

The passage above comes from chapter 8, which returns to the by now familiar style of Bloom's interior monologue, following him as he walks the Dublin streets at one o'clock in search for a place to eat. His hunger, and the theme of food, dominate the chapter, which is named 'Lestrygonians' after Homer's cannibal giants. At this point, however, the sight of a pub that was once a music hall has prompted memories of an earlier stage of his marriage. The first paragraph is made up entirely of Bloom's thoughts, some in complete sentences, some just fragments. There is nothing here like Stephen's poetic imagination, though Bloom's mental language has a poetry of its own. His sense of past happiness immediately, and typically, leads him to a brief mental exploration of the question of identity, 'Or was that I? Or am I now I?', a question that Stephen is later to mull over more philosophically. We then learn something important about the sexual history of the Blooms that will be developed later in the book: since the death of their infant son Rudy eleven years before they have not had complete sexual intercourse. It is characteristic of the novel that this information is conveyed in a passing thought, among a multitude of other passing thoughts; typical too is the uncertainty about the implied pronoun in 'Could never like it again after Rudy'. Was it Bloom or Molly who was turned off sex – or both of them? Bloom, of course, knows what he means, but Joyce leaves it to the reader to puzzle it out – and critics still disagree.

The mood of pathos and resignation in Bloom's comments and questions about the past is lightened when his mind turns to his current source of sexual stimulation, Martha Clifford, the writer of the letter he picked up from the post office earlier that morning. Martha, too, had asked a question about his happiness, and the exact words cross Bloom's mind: 'Are you not happy in your home you poor little naughty boy?' Once more, Joyce relies on our memory to make the link between Bloom's thought and the words of the letter. Without making it, we would be baffled by the sentences that follow, in which Bloom resolves to reply to Martha's letter in the library. (In fact he does so, as we shall see, in a hotel dining room.)

The second paragraph begins with a third-person narrative: a colourful description of Dublin's foremost shopping street at the start of the century, with some inventive hyphenless compounds from the narrator to intensify the evocation of both sights and sounds. But it soon gives way to interior monologue again – signalled by content and syntactic incompleteness: 'Thick feet that woman has in the white stockings.' Bloom always has an eye for women's legs, and now he is severe upon a woman who is clearly from the country and has made the mistake – in his eyes – of wearing white stockings. Even Molly, it seems, doesn't look her best in them. To the alert reader, there is another echo of a letter quoted earlier in the book, this time one written to Bloom by his fifteen-year-old daughter Milly, who is working in a photographic studio in Mullingar, fifty miles from Dublin. She had commented that on fair day 'all the beef to the heels were in' – an odd use of a phrase that usually refers to a woman with thick ankles (which is clearly the association it has for Bloom). Bloom will later remember the woman in Grafton Street, contrasting her unappealing white stockings with the transparent stockings worn by a girl who has deliberately aroused him on the beach, and again the phrase will cross his mind (13.931–2). This curious thread continues on to the fourteenth episode, in which a student Milly has met in Mullingar turns up in Dublin in the company of Buck Mulligan and refers to her, approvingly, as 'big of her age and beef to the heel' (14.502–3). This is just one of the hundreds of strands of repeated phrases woven through the book, producing the simple pleasure of recognition each time they occur, conveying the way phrases unaccountably stick in one's mind or come back to one unexpectedly, and tying different episodes together in a complex unity.

There is something else going on in this paragraph of which Bloom is unaware. Just as the headlines in 'Aeolus' are not uttered or thought by any of the characters, and are not even part of the narrative, so in many of the episodes the choice of words, including the words characters utter, is in part determined by the Homeric parallel rather than by any individual motivation. 'Lestrygonians' is peppered with food terms, both in references to food or eating (much of the chapter concerns Bloom's lunch) and in phrases that have little connection with food except through metaphor or pun. The word Bloom chooses for 'yokel' is 'chawbacon'; he thinks of Molly as out of 'plumb' in white stockings; and Milly's phrase 'beef to the heels' comes into his mind. In a different chapter, Bloom might have used other terms – in 'Lotus-Eaters', for example, which is full of flower terms, he might have thought of the country woman as a 'hayseed'. If the reader expects everything in the text to serve the purpose of the story being told, this added layer will seem irrelevant or even irritating;

but if it is enjoyed as yet another dimension of the play of language, and one that contributes to the distinctiveness of each chapter, it can provide much amusement. There's no doubt that it plays havoc with traditional ideas of character, however: if we were to say that Bloom thinks of an opera by Meyerbeer because of the last syllable of the composer's name, we would be confusing the careful delineation of his personality with the verbal games being played in a completely different realm, one that is wholly outside the imagined world Bloom is living in. (It might be argued that the food and drink terms come to him because he is hungry and thirsty: apart from the somewhat dubious psychology of this argument, it wouldn't extend to the examples in other chapters such as the references to flowers in 'Lotus-Eaters' or to eyes and blindness in 'Cyclops'.)

There *is* psychological accuracy, and readerly pleasure, in the wonderful inventiveness that leads Bloom from one thought to another. The lavish display of poplin in the windows of Brown Thomas (a real store in Grafton Street in 1904) reminds him that poplin was introduced into Ireland by the Huguenots – the sort of factual detail that Bloom's head is stuffed with.[10] We can guess this fact from the text, but spotting the next connection depends on a certain amount of musical knowledge: Meyerbeer wrote a popular opera entitled *The Huguenots*, and Bloom proceeds to sing bits of it to himself (not getting it quite right, which is also typical of him). In the middle of his little performance, however, he reverts to the washing instructions for poplin in the window in front of him.

Then an external stimulus – pincushions in the shop window – again prompts a chain of thought. The interior monologue becomes fragmented here, but it is not difficult to deduce that underneath the musings about poplin and opera Bloom is still thinking about Molly. It is to her that he has addressed the threat that he will buy a pincushion, as she sticks pins all over the place, or leaves needles in curtains. Turning back to the window display doesn't help him take his mind off the impending adultery: petticoats and stockings bring back thoughts of female sexuality, and with them the conviction that the afternoon visit Blazes Boylan will make to the Blooms' house is not purely for singing practice. There is nothing preventing Bloom from returning home and thwarting the planned assignation – nothing except his sense that it is inevitable. In these few words – 'Useless to go back. Had to be.' – we have the mainspring of the book's action: Bloom spends the day in wanderings around Dublin in order not to go home, in comic contrast to Odysseus' wanderings around the Mediterranean in an attempt, constantly thwarted by the gods, to get home. Much of his activity, physical and mental, is dedicated to avoiding even thinking about Molly and Boylan – though events constantly conspire against him to provide reminders. Yet it is not an entirely negative scenario: there are hints that Bloom finds some erotic fulfilment in the thought of Molly's sexual encounter with another man. This idea is given full-frontal staging in the 'Circe' episode (though we must be cautious about interpreting this unproblematically as Bloom's hidden desire), and Molly herself reveals in the 'Penelope' episode her suspicion that Bloom has got Milly out of the house to make her adultery possible.

Whatever the complex balance of dismay and desire, the third of the three short phrases, 'Tell me all', signals more than just a longing for Molly to be honest with him: it could equally indicate a desire to hear about her sexual activity in detail, an alternative strengthened by the fact that it is an echo in Bloom's mind of another phrase from Martha's letter – one that undoubtedly had an erotic charge in that context. It is in these delicate tracings of emotion, memory and desire that Joyce's technique of interior monologue shows itself

to be a highly effective tool in achieving a degree of realism un-
matched even by the great nineteenth-century novelists.
However, realism is not his only aim, and though it comes as
a surprise at first, his abandonment of interior monologue for
the larger part of what remains of the book enables him to test
the limited goals of his predecessors and provide the reader
with several new kinds of entertainment.

6

ULYSSES III: MUSICAL WORDS

By Bachelor's walk jogjaunty jingled Blazes Boylan, bachelor, in sun in heat, mare's glossy rump atrot, with flick of whip, on bounding tyres: sprawled, warmseated, Boylan impatience, ardentbold. Horn. Have you the? Horn. Have you the? Haw haw horn.

Over their voices Dollard bassooned attack, booming over bombarding chords:

—*When love absorbs my ardent soul . . .*

Roll of Bensoulbenjamin rolled to the quivery loveshivery roofpanes.

—War! War! cried Father Cowley. You're the warrior.

—So I am, Ben Warrior laughed. I was thinking of your landlord. Love or money.

He stopped. He wagged huge beard, huge face over his blunder huge.

—Sure, you'd burst the tympanum of her ear, man, Mr Dedalus said through smoke aroma, with an organ like yours.

In bearded abundant laughter Dollard shook upon the keyboard. He would.

—Not to mention another membrane, Father Cowley added.

Ulysses, 11.524–40

From Bloom's lunch in 'Lestrygonians' the novel moves to Stephen's literary ambitions in 'Scylla and Charybdis', episode 9, which takes place in the National Library of Ireland from 2 p.m., and replaces Odysseus' dangerous passage between the monsters of the rock and the whirlpool with Stephen's mental negotiation between the forces of Aristotelian pragmatism and Platonic idealism. This shift from bodily to intellectual activity is part of the many-layered patterning by which the two characters – Leopold, a father who has lost a son, and Stephen, a son who needs a better father than his biological one – are related, both by opposites and parallels. (The narrator of the 'Ithaca' episode calls them, at one point, 'Stoom' and 'Blephen' [17.549, 551]). After Stephen tries, without much success, to persuade the literary elite of Dublin of his merits as writer and critic, he experiences another near-encounter with Bloom, who is in the library in pursuit of his ad. The following chapter, 'Wandering Rocks', visits a number of sites around Dublin, pausing on several characters in addition to the three chief ones, Leopold, Stephen and Molly, who are thus viewed in the context of the continuing life of Dublin – or at least of a particular segment of its population. When he does give us vignettes of Stephen and Bloom, it is to show the former acknowledging the painful circumstances of his family in an encounter with one of his sisters and the latter purchasing a book entitled *Sweets of Sin* for Molly (a book that will provide many repeated motifs in later episodes). By intercutting the various scenes, Joyce highlights the simultaneity of the events depicted and the impossibility of their being truly captured in a linear narrative; he also reprises the panoramic effect of *Dubliners*, showing men and women engrossed in their attempts to make a living in a society that discourages free thought, expression and political choice. To provide a sense of the dominant powers in Dublin, Joyce traces two journeys through the streets of the city, that of a Catholic priest, Father Conmee, and that of the Lord Lieutenant, the King's representative in Ireland; and to bring their eminence down a peg or two, he gives us the responses of ordinary Dubliners to their spiritual and political masters.

The passage above comes from the eleventh episode, named 'Sirens' after the enchanting singers who lure men to their death, but whom Odysseus manages to hear in safety by having his men bind him to his ship's mast. Joyce's sirens are two barmaids in the Ormond Hotel, and we see a number of their victims fall prey to their sexual charms (in a very mild way). Bloom watches them with some degree of arousal, but is safely taken up with his own dalliance as he chooses this moment to pen his reply to Martha. There is a particular reason for Bloom's decision to undertake this absorbing task now: the chapter begins at 4 p.m., the time of Blazes Boylan's assignation with Molly. The chapter also provides a compelling vignette of the popular inheritance of romantic Irish nationalism – later to be fully explored in the 'Cyclops' episode – by having the patriotic Irish ballad 'The Croppy Boy' sung with intense feeling in the saloon. Joyce refuses to take the sacred texts of Irish nationalism entirely seriously, however, and allows Bloom's reading of Robert Emmet's famous speech from the dock to be accompanied by the chapter's final musical utterance, our hero's fart.

Not only does 'Sirens' mark a turning point in Bloom's and Molly's day; it marks a turning point in the adventures of language that the novel has embarked upon. The episode begins with a list of brief phrases, experienced as sound as much as sense, which turn out to be fragments of the chapter to come; sometimes called the 'overture', it is more like a symphony orchestra's period of tuning, when you might hear scraps of the work about to be played. The action of the chapter moves freely among different sites, as 'Wandering Rocks' had done in a more elaborate way; at first between the interior of the bar, where the barmaids are taking their tea, and the quays of the River Liffey, where Bloom is walking with food on his mind once more. Seeing Boylan go into the Ormond Hotel, Bloom cannot resist following; his plan is to sit in the dining room near the door and watch him without being seen – once again, he isn't sure whether he desires or dreads what is about to happen. Boylan remains in the bar, flirting with the barmaids and drinking sloe gin, and then sets off in his hackney car, without having noticed that Bloom is in the room next door. Meanwhile Simon Dedalus, Stephen's father, plays the piano in the saloon, after which he tries to persuade one of his companions, Ben Dollard, to sing. Bloom tucks into the liver and bacon he has ordered. The passage above follows.

It begins with a glimpse of Boylan on his way. There is no difficulty in understanding the meaning of this paragraph: it is a vividly realized description of Molly's lover-to-be as sexual conqueror, excited by the prospect of his erotic adventure. But Joyce's technique is far from straightforward. The first sentence takes a fairly simple statement, 'Blazes Boylan jingled by Bachelor's Walk', rearranges it, and expands it by means of words and phrases to produce an intense evocation of sound, vision, motion and erotic energy. Some of the words are made up – 'jogjaunty', 'warmseated', 'ardentbold' – and some of the phrases defy grammatical analysis – 'mare's glossy rump atrot', 'Boylan impatience'. Even words that refer to the mare or the hackney car or the weather are suffused with Boylan's arousal: 'heat', 'rump', 'bounding'. The chapter has already begun to play with Boylan's name, and to make a constantly varying refrain out of his mode of transport, a jaunting car with jingling springs, always with sexual suggestiveness. Thus when Bloom sees Boylan's carriage and decides on an impulse to follow it, Joyce writes 'Jingling on supple rubbers it jaunted from the bridge to Ormond quay' (11.304–5) (The word 'jingle' has also become inseparable from the image of Molly in bed, ever since, in the 'Calypso' episode, 'she turned over and the loose brass quoits of the bedstead jingled' [4.59].) A joke made by one of the characters in 'Wandering Rocks' – 'Tell him I'm Boylan with impatience' (10.486) – is taken up in this episode by the text itself: Lenehan, we are told, 'waited for Boylan with impatience, for jinglejaunty blazes boy' (11.289–90); then the joke is repeated when Boylan announces his departure (11.426); and now we have an abbreviated version of the same joke. These verbal games – though they may echo the wit of Simon Dedalus and his friends – can't be said to be invented by anyone within the narrative frame: in 'Sirens' Joyce's language begins to take a leading part, which it will not relinquish for the remainder of the book. The effects it is capable of include moments of hilarity, pathos, earnestness, recklessness and eroticism: and although the characters share in these emotions, the words convey them directly to the reader without the question 'Who is expressing these feelings?' being of central importance.

There is also perhaps a hint that Bloom is imagining Boylan at this moment, with dismay but perhaps with some excitement as well. One clue to this depends on our recognizing an echo of a thought of Bloom's from a few minutes earlier. As he passes Boylan's carriage outside the hotel, which his rival has entered a moment before, he thinks 'The seat he sat on: warm' (11.342). Bloom is looking at the seat of the carriage and imagining the warmth it has retained from Boylan's bum: a strangely intimate response that bespeaks Bloom's fascination with the other man's physical being, even if it is tinged with revulsion. Now we have 'warmseated', which we may simply take as the text's own echo of Bloom's thought, or we may feel that it associates this paragraph with Bloom's thoughts and emotions.

The jokes in this passage are many, and their corniness is not inappropriate in the description of a character who is almost a parody of the rakish lover. Joyce uses his favoured technique of repetition to signal the aptness of the street Boylan is travelling along (and Bachelor's Walk is, as one would expect, a real street near the Ormond Hotel). The joke about 'boiling with impatience' can, as we've seen, now be abbreviated, since we've heard it before; while 'ardent-bold' is a proleptic joke, linking the description of Boylan to the song Dollard is about to sing. And the joke that combines Boylan's horniness and Bloom's cuckold's horns in a call-and-response sequence is built out of Lenehan's earlier ribald comment on Boylan's haste to leave the hotel: 'Got the horn or what?' (We've had advance notice in the episode's opening sequence, which includes the fragment 'Horn. Hawhorn.' [11.23]). This joke also provides a further instance of the play with thematically appropriate words we noted in the 'Lestrygonians' passage: the continuous theme of 'Sirens' is, of course, music, and Lenehan is unconsciously participating in the texture of musical terms when he uses a word which happens also to be the name of a musical instrument. (We can fit 'jingled' into the same pattern.)

The remainder of the passage deals directly with music. One of the pleasures of 'Sirens' is Joyce's convincing depiction of an afternoon gathering of male Dubliners in a bar, characterized by repartee and music-making. Several songs are sung during this hour, and there is some solo piano-playing as well. Simon Dedalus has asked Ben Dollard, who is at the piano and whose bass voice is well known to his companions, to give a rendition of 'Love and War', a duet representing the contrast between these two all-consuming passions. Joyce's verbal inventiveness is again evident in his descriptive words 'bassooned', 'booming' and 'bombarding', the last word being particularly apt, since a 'bombard' is both a cannon (from which the familiar verb comes) and a deep wooden instrument of the bassoon family. By this stage of the novel, the somewhat excessive alliteration comes over not as authorial clumsiness but as a comic comment on the use of this technique for poetic purposes. Even more inventive is the sentence that follows Dollard's beginning of the song: 'Roll of Bensoulbenjamin rolled to the quivery loveshivery roofpanes.' The words of the song are taken up into the description of its sounds as they rise to the ceiling, and Joyce includes repetition and rhyme to emphasize the musicality of the language.

But Dollard has sung the wrong words in his huge bass voice: he is supposed to be singing of war, not love, as Cowley reminds him. The reader should have no difficulty in following Dollard's response, as not many pages have been turned since a conversation between him and Cowley in which the name of the latter's landlord came up: the Reverend Mr Love (10.948). Hence, too, the joke about 'love or money': as we learned then, Cowley is in arrears with his rent. The rechristening of Dollard as 'Ben Warrior' that follows is typical of the episode's antics; in fact, characters' names first started being infected by their verbal context in 'Scylla and Charybdis'. Then once again there is a strong contrast between the believable colloquial language of the speakers and the distortions of the narrative voice: Joyce removes the articles and repeats the word 'huge' to convey all the more powerfully Dollard's size; as, a little later, the size of his laugh, and the way it animates his face, is brought out by the adjectives 'bearded abundant', with their striking sound pattern.

Simon's jocular response to Dollard's mistake involves two more musical instruments appropriate to the chapter's theme, drum and organ, though their primary meanings here are physiological, not musical. Cowley provides a sexual extension of the joke, and the reader using an annotated edition will be told that there is a reference here, on Joyce's part if not

Cowley's, to the tradition that the Virgin Mary conceived through the ear. We may doubt the relevance of this somewhat recherché allusion, but our doubts won't last any further than the 'Circe' episode, where we find a bizarre materialization of Bloom's grandfather asserting that a Roman centurion impregnated Mary, and continuing: 'Messiah! He burst her tympanum' (at which point the figure of Ben Dollard appears on the scene yodelling 'When love absorbs my ardent soul') (15.2599–610). The more one reads Joyce, the less one is willing to call an allusion too obscure or a connection too distant, whether it is a reference to elite European culture or the popular knowledge of the streets and bars.

7

ULYSSES IV: THE PLAY'S THE THING

FATHER MALACHI O'FLYNN
(*takes from the chalice and elevates a blooddripping host*) *Corpus meum.*

THE REVEREND MR HAINES LOVE
(*raises high behind the celebrant's petticoat, revealing his grey bare hairy buttocks between which a carrot is stuck*) My body.

THE VOICE OF ALL THE DAMNED
Htengier Tnetopinmo Dog Drol eht rof, Aiulella!

(*From on high the voice of Adonai calls.*)

ADONAI
Doooooooooooog!

THE VOICE OF ALL THE BLESSED
Alleluia, for the Lord God Omnipotent reigneth!

(*From on high the voice of Adonai calls.*)

ADONAI
Goooooooooooood!

(*In strident discord peasants and townsmen of Orange and Green factions sing* Kick the Pope *and* Daily, daily sing to Mary.)

PRIVATE CARR
(*with ferocious articulation*) I'll do him in, so help me fucking

Christ! I'll wring the bastard fucker's bleeding blasted fucking
windpipe!

Ulysses 15.4702–21

A short extract from 'Circe' can give only the merest taste of
this mad extravaganza, going on for 150 pages and involving
scenes of such cornucopian excess that any Hollywood director would be envious. From 'Sirens', the episodes have grown
longer and more stylistically extreme, but 'Circe' is the longest
and most outrageous. The episode immediately after 'Sirens',
the twelfth, continues the lifelike representation of Dublin
public house conversation, and like 'Sirens' it contrasts this
witty, often scabrous, talk with passages of extraordinary literary inventiveness. The difference is that in this episode, which
Joyce called 'Cyclops' after the one-eyed giants of the *Odyssey*,
passages of realistic interaction offered to us with colloquial
bravado by a nameless narrator alternate with inflated parodies
of a series of different types of heightened language. The
events of the chapter reflect again Bloom's outsider status: the
mistaken belief that he has correctly predicted the winner of
the Gold Cup and pocketed his winnings results in a great
deal of hostility, culminating in a hasty escape at the climax of
the chapter. Anti-Semitism and narrow nationalist opinions
are the monocular attitudes the chapter pillories, and Joyce
suggests that they spring from a common source. At the same
time, the notion that universal love is the answer is not spared
mockery.

'Nausicaa', which follows (after a two-hour gap which is
never completely accounted for), is Joyce's rewriting of the
scene in which the naked Odysseus, cast up on the beach,
wins the good graces of the princess Nausicaa. In this version,
the princess is a young Dublin woman, Gerty MacDowell, sit-
ting on a rock on Sandymount beach while her friends play
with their younger siblings. Noticing a stranger – we guess

that it is Bloom – looking at her, she offers him an eyeful of
her underwear; and, realizing that the sight has prompted him
to masturbate (though she doesn't use and probably doesn't
know the word), she reveals more and more of her upper
thighs, until his orgasm coincides with the bursting overhead
of fireworks from a nearby bazaar. Just as striking as the content is the style: Joyce parodies the kind of women's magazine
or cheap fiction Gerty presumably reads, though with
repeated moments of bathos as the more down-to-earth side
of her personality asserts itself. The style doesn't attempt to
transcribe Gerty's thoughts – it is not a version of interior
monologue – but to present her thoughts in the kind of language that she might regard as appropriately literary. The
second half of the chapter shifts to the detumescent Bloom, in
the familiar mode of interior monologue, who notices, as
Gerty leaves the scene, that she has a limp.

'Oxen of the Sun', episode 14, is perhaps the one at which
readers are most likely to balk. Not only is the language
unusually dense – even for *Ulysses* – but not a great deal happens (even though it is the chapter in which Stephen and
Bloom finally achieve a proper meeting, the chapter for which
a conventional novel would have pulled out all the stops).
Bloom makes his way to the Holles Street Maternity Hospital
to enquire after an acquaintance, Mina Purefoy, who has been
in labour for three days. There he is invited to join a group of
medical students and their friends – including Stephen – who
are having an animated conversation over beer, bread and sar-
dines. Mulligan and Bannon (the student from Mullingar)
join them later. The conversation has a lot to do with fertility and its containment (Joyce said that the killing by
Odysseus' men of the sun-god's cattle was mirrored in the act
of contraception), and, as one might imagine, words having to
do with cows and bulls (including a Papal Bull) are freely
employed. What makes the episode a challenge for the reader,

however, is that Joyce wrote it as a series of parodies, in chronological order, of the historical styles of written English, until the final section, which is in a kind of modern spoken multicultural demotic. The young men – and Bloom – are by this stage in a pub, and we hear Stephen suggesting to his friend Lynch that they head for the brothel area of Dublin across the river. Bloom hears them, too, and his actions for the next few hours are governed by his solicitude for Stephen, whose unusual abilities, and need of something like paternal support, he senses.

The enchantress Circe turns men into animals; only the wily Odysseus, protected by a herb recommended to him by Hermes, is immune. As a result, he undoes her power, removes the spell from her victims, and lives for a year as her guest. Her equivalent in the 'Circe' episode is Bella Cohen, the madam of the brothel to which the very drunk Stephen and his companion Lynch repair, and to which they are traced by Bloom – who is now full of concern at the young man's state. What protects the modern Odysseus from the sexual enchantment of the brothel, it seems, is his lack of sexual desire, attributable to his recent masturbation.

The transformations that characterize the chapter start from the very beginning: the prose narrative is turned into a bizarre play, and the setting is luridly described in a series of detailed but completely unworkable stage directions. Any person, present or absent, any animal, any object, can be given the status of a character and assigned a speech. The chapter is often spoken of as a tissue of hallucinations, and it is certainly hallucinatory; but it is not clear who might be hallucinating. In a way, it is a place where the book itself indulges in fantastic revisions of its earlier relatively sober descriptions and speeches. Much of it seems to be an elaboration of Bloom's desires and guilt (and much guilty desire), but it would be unwise to say that it reveals the 'truth' of his psyche.

There is, however, sufficient distinction between those passages that represent the actions and conversations in the street and within Bella Cohen's brothel and those that take off into a phantasmagorical stratosphere to enable the attentive reader to trace a narrative thread. The most significant events are Bloom's discovery of Stephen and Lynch in the brothel, Stephen's terrified encounter with a hallucinated ghostly mother (here we do seem to be in the realm of genuine psychic experience), his subsequent smashing of a paper lampshade, and his altercation with two British privates outside the brothel, one of whom knocks him out. We also see Bloom paying for the damage Stephen has done to the lamp, and managing to ward off the attentions of two policemen after the fracas. The chapter ends with a final impossible vision: Bloom, standing next to the prostrate form of the barely conscious young man he has treated with fatherly care, sees his dead son, Rudy, aged eleven as he would be if he had lived, reading a book from right to left.

How do we read a passage like the one at the head of this chapter? For a start, the recognition factor is stronger in 'Circe' than in any other episode: we are constantly meeting familiar figures, reading familiar phrases, hearing distorted echoes of what has gone before. But there is also the pleasure of the transformations: in this passage, Malachi Mulligan, who in the opening sentences of the book was introduced performing a mock mass with his shaving bowl as chalice, is now combined with the titular hero of a well-known ballad, referred to a couple of times earlier, to become Father Malachi O'Flynn (and perhaps we hear an echo of Father Flynn from 'The Sisters'); while his English companion, Haines, fuses with Father Cowley's landlord, familiar from the 'Wandering Rocks' and 'Sirens' episodes, to become the Reverend Mr Haines Love. But we are bound to ask ourselves of this passage, and a multitude of others in this episode that are equally bizarre, 'What is really going on?' We have arrived at this point from the very realistic quarrel between Stephen and the two soldiers, via an extraordinary page-long apocalyptic stage direction, in which Dublin burns, the earth trembles, dragons' teeth turn into armed warriors, duels are fought, and finally there rises an altarstone on which the naked body of Mina Purefoy lies, 'a chalice resting on her swollen belly' (another phrase that hints at a connection with 'The Sisters'). Not only can we not imagine any of this actually happening, or being staged; we cannot imagine anyone imagining it – except Joyce. Just as the verbal antics of 'Sirens' or the gigantic parodies of 'Cyclops' can't be thought of as emanating from anyone in the world of the novel, so these strange scenes seem to be the product of a creative force well beyond the characters living their lives in Dublin in 1904. Our enjoyment of the book will be thwarted if we constantly try to tie such elements down to the reality of the fictional world; but it will be considerably enhanced if we can share some of the exuberance and hilarity of these wild outbursts of parodic and exhibitionist language.

It is not difficult to identify the scene at the start of the passage as a black mass, the inverted Christian ritual long associated with Satan-worship. The host is dripping with blood, instead of undergoing transubstantiation; the praise of God is recited backwards; and the voice of Adonai utters 'Doooooooooooog!' instead of the reverse. The carrot sticking out of Mulligan's backside speaks for itself. Mulligan's mocking attitude towards religion, evident from the first episode, is now concretized in an impossible and exaggerated event; and in case we start to take it too seriously, the alarming but also hilarious sight of those 'grey bare hairy buttocks' with their vegetable ornament is enough to banish any lingering sobriety. By this point of the chapter, not far from its end, we have become fairly accustomed to unlikely personages in the playscript, but it is still a surprise to find 'the voice of all the damned' speaking the words of the reverse mass. In all Joyce's work, religion, and the Catholic religion in particular, comes in for a rough ride; here, however, hostility towards religion is shown as being in danger of turning into a perverted religion itself.

The reversed incantations are followed by a pleasing restitution of the proper order from the mouths of the blessed, and the correct pronunciation of the divine name, albeit extended by the proliferating o's to something a little less than reverent. Readers with some Biblical knowledge – or access to annotations – will know that the words of the blessed are those uttered at the Last Judgement, according to Revelations; and of course the separation of the damnèd and the blessed indicate the same eschatological scene. This being Ireland, however, the name of God does not produce harmony; it results in a singing match between Protestant and Catholic factions, the former adopting an Orange chant, the latter a pious hymn.

Then, without warning, we are back with a character who has his feet on solid Dublin soil. Private Carr, although his existence on the page is typographically identical to that of Father Malachi O'Flynn and the voice of all the damned, is a flesh-and-blood individual, and shows no awareness of the mayhem that we have been reading about since his last utterance. He is still enraged at Stephen (whose drunken, but still highly intellectual, words he has not been able to make any sense of), and Joyce is nothing if not realistic in his recording of the soldier's speech. That Private Carr is English – one can hear his English accent in his foulmouthed bluster – is significant: his presence on the streets of Dublin is a reminder that this is a city under constant military surveillance, and although the fight between the drunken Irishman and the not-too-bright Englishman is more comic than anything else, it carries some weight in the larger picture of the city's political and social oppression.

'Circe', then, exploits the enormous fertility of language freed from its usual constraints by the demands of representational accuracy. If it is not representing something or, more importantly, not even pretending to represent something (which is what fiction usually does), but rather bringing whatever seems most funny, most sensational, most fantastic into being, it offers us a similar pleasure in opening our minds to images and verbal constructions we would not have dreamed of unaided. Other literary works that engage with the powers and dangers of the imagination as it explores the further reaches of desire, sex, guilt and jealousy – Proust's *Sodome et Gomorrhe* comes to mind as an example contemporary with *Ulysses* – seem sober by comparison. If there are constraints in effect from time to time, they have to do with the episode's reinvention of everything that we have so far read, though once again we must not be too literal-minded. When Gerty MacDowell limps onto the Circean stage showing Bloom her 'bloodied clout', this may be a comment on conventional attitudes towards female virginity but it has nothing to do with what the real Gerty might be doing at this hour.

This expansive riot of colour, sound, activity, speech, song, sex, rage, remorse and ceaseless transformation is held in check by the simple device of the playscript layout: no matter what is happening or being said, it comes to us within the confines of upper case, centred character names, italicized stage directions, and speeches of varying lengths. Without this mode of control, it might be unreadable; but as it stands, it is one of the highlights of the book, and of European fiction.

8

ULYSSES V: MOLLY BLOOM AT HOME

I suppose I oughtnt to have buried him in that little woolly jacket I knitted crying as I was but give it to some poor child but I knew well Id never have another our 1st death too it was we were never the same since O Im not going to think myself into the glooms about that any more I wonder why he wouldnt stay the night I felt all the time it was somebody strange he brought in instead of roving around the city meeting God knows who nightwalkers and pickpockets his poor mother wouldnt like that if she was alive ruining himself for life perhaps still its a lovely hour so silent I used to love coming home after dances the air of the night they have friends they can talk to weve none either he wants what he wont get or its some woman ready to stick her knife in you I hate that in women no wonder they treat us the way they do we are a dreadful lot of bitches

Ulysses 18.1448–59

After 'Circe' has granted Bloom a vision of his son Rudy, the book enters its final phase: the 'Nostos', or homecoming. Just as Odysseus returned to his home on the island of Ithaca, where he was aided by the swineherd Eumaeus, slew the suitors who had been pestering Penelope, and was reunited with his son and his wife, so Bloom returns – with a stop en route for refreshment in a cabmen's shelter – to number 7 Eccles Street, finds a way of dealing with what is now the certainty of Molly's adultery, and joins his wife in bed. Stephen, who has accompanied Bloom back to his home, does not play the Telemachus role to the end, however, refusing the offer of accommodation and walking into the night. This is all played out across three long chapters, known from Joyce's schema as 'Eumaeus', 'Ithaca' and 'Penelope'.

'Eumaeus', chapter 16, is one of the funniest episodes to read once the long-windedness of the writing is appreciated as a wicked parody of the kind of well-meaning but cliché-ridden and self-important public discourse of the time, like that of a bad leader-writer or a pompous, error-prone politician. The contrast with the kaleidoscopic variety of 'Circe' couldn't be greater. In this chapter, Stephen and Bloom at last effect some kind of union. While walking, and in the cabmen's shelter, they converse at length – or at least Bloom does, Stephen's responses being much less verbose. Bloom conceives a plan to have Stephen living with him and Molly, and the thought of a possible sexual relationship between the young man and his wife is not entirely absent from his mind, nor is it entirely unappealing to him. However, nothing is wholly trustworthy in this episode, which takes its character from the episode in the *Odyssey* where the hero wears a disguise to deceive his enemies (and even his faithful swineherd).

The following chapter, 'Ithaca', invents yet another style, one of the most original in the book. It is made up entirely of questions and answers, and exhibits a gleeful unpredictability in both the particular questions being asked and the ways in which they are answered. The language tends towards the scientific and rational, though with some moving transitions into more poetic phrasing. Through the mass of detail – to be read for its own sake, not in the hope that it will move the story along – we can just discern a sequence of events: Bloom and Stephen walk back to Eccles Street, where Bloom makes cocoa for them both in the kitchen, the conversation blossoms (Stephen, it seems, now taking a full part in it), the offer of a made-up bed is declined and, after the two of them pee in the yard, Stephen leaves. The moment the narrative had seemed to be leading towards, the bonding of its Telemachus and its Odysseus, doesn't arrive; but there has been a union of sorts, and the older man's kindness registers strongly on the reader and, we must assume, on Stephen. Bloom then makes his way to bed (noting that the furniture has been rearranged), where Molly is asleep amid signs of her earlier sexual endeavours – something Bloom is able to absorb with remarkable equanimity. He kisses her on the bottom, tells her about his day (with some strategic omissions), then falls asleep.

At first sight, the final chapter, 'Penelope', is one of the most forbidding. It presents the reader with a solid block of text, paragraphs several pages long, and a complete absence of punctuation marks.[11] In fact, it is one of the most immediately accessible of the episodes: it doesn't take long to get used to the absence of punctuation, and although one often has to adjust one's interpretation of a particular phrase on discovering that it goes with the one after rather than the one before, Molly's thought processes come through clearly and colourfully. (Sometimes it is not clear who she's referring to when she says 'he', but this ambiguity – which is not an ambiguity for Molly, of course – contributes to the feeling of her generous erotic interest in the opposite sex.) There is plenty to keep readers on their toes, though, especially in the details that offer a fresh perspective on the world according to Bloom – the version that has so far been the dominant one. To take a fairly trivial example, albeit one with an important Homeric pedigree, we have been led to believe from one of Bloom's first stretches of interior monologue that the bed they are in was bought in Gibraltar 'at the governor's auction' (4.62); now we learn that this has been a fib of Molly's to impress Bloom, and that in fact, far from being Lord Napier's bed, it was bought from 'old Cohen', who 'scratched himself in it often enough' (18.1213). (Odysseus proves his identity to Penelope through his knowledge of the secret of their bed's construction.)

Molly's thoughts rove over the events of the afternoon, her past (and in particular her sexual experiences as a girl), possibilities for the future (including her next rendezvous with Boylan and Stephen's promise as a potential lover), and her husband's peculiarities and peccadilloes. Her language is frank, physical, full of energetic delight or disgust. She frequently contradicts herself. Although she thinks hungrily about sex with Boylan, and has a good laugh at many of Bloom's behavioural oddities, there emerges a sense that, after all is said and done, she rates her husband above all the other men in her life, past and present.

In terms of action, very little happens. Bloom, it seems, has asked for his breakfast in bed the following morning, and Molly, accustomed as she is to being ministered to by her husband at this hour, is amazed; she guesses that he has come somewhere but, unsurprisingly, is in the dark about where. (The reader, of course, remembers his masturbation.) She farts, as quietly as she can, her period arrives, she uses the chamber pot, fetches a napkin from the press, and returns to bed (where she and her husband lie, as they customarily do, and as Joyce and Nora are said to have done, the one's head next to the other's feet). All this time her mind is whirling, giving us a view of the Blooms' marriage, and the Dublin society they move in, that complements and complicates the picture we have already received over seventeen episodes. Sex is, of course, on her mind, and Joyce brushes aside the fierce taboos of the time to evoke in unconstrained terms the mental and physical delight in reliving and imagining a range of sexual experiences.

As the passage above indicates, the visual effect of the absence of punctuation is of thoughts moving pell-mell in one direction then another, a very different effect from the allusive intellectual sweeps of Stephen's thinking or the disjointed probing of Bloom's. However, we can't assume that Molly's way of thinking is entirely distinct from that of the other characters; what Joyce is showing us is how two very different stylistic techniques can each convey the impression of spontaneous thought. Both are illusions, using their deviation from the norms of written language to suggest to the reader a different kind of language from the one we usually employ. They convey the flavour of distinctive personalities and situations, and this run-on style seems particularly appropriate to night thoughts that develop according to their own associative logic rather than in response to external stimuli.

Early readers who reached the final episode and overcame the forbidding look of the pages to immerse themselves in Molly's mental universe were often surprised at what they found. One reviewer in 1922, after describing the typographical oddity of the chapter, commented: 'Mr. Joyce evidently believes in making it difficult for his readers – but perhaps he wants to scare them away. I am bound to admit, however, that this chapter, perhaps the best in the book, and one of the most disgusting, is by no means as difficult to read as one might expect.'[12] Another one admits that Molly's monologue is 'the vilest, according to ordinary standards, in all literature' but goes on: 'And yet its very obscenity is somehow beautiful.'[13] More recently, there has been much debate about the sexual politics of a male author who adopts a female voice to articulate what could be seen as a stereotype of feminine garrulity, contradictoriness and earthiness. The opposing argument – that Joyce offers a critique of female stereotypes while relishing their potential for comedy, often at the expense of male vanity and short-sightedness – is a strong one, however, particularly if one judges Joyce against the standards of the time.

Molly, like her husband, has been profoundly affected by the death of Rudy, and can't help thinking of the woollen jacket she had knitted for him before he died and that he was buried in. (In the vision of Rudy at the end of 'Circe', a 'white lambkin peeps out of his waistcoat pocket' [15.4967].) Here we have Molly's version of the change in their relationship that Rudy's death caused – both her own sense that she would never have another child and the admission that 'we were never the same since'. This statement provides, perhaps, the preposition that was missing from Bloom's incomplete sentence in 'Lestrygonians', 'Could never like it again after Rudy'. But it is characteristic of Molly that she can rouse herself from the 'glooms', and the next thing we know she is thinking about Stephen. Bloom has told her of Stephen's refusal of the offer of hospitality and, rather like the reader, she finds this odd. It takes a moment to untangle Molly's syntax here as she first comments on her earlier sense that the person Bloom had brought into the house was a relative stranger and then reverts to her bafflement at his departure; the complete sentence about Stephen is: 'I wonder why he wouldn't stay the night instead of roving around the city meeting God knows who, nightwalkers and pickpockets.' At this point, Molly's interest in Stephen is protective and motherly; later in her monologue it will become more erotically charged. She has heard, of course, of Stephen's mother's death even though she clearly isn't a friend of the family – there is a strong sense throughout the novel of a community of Dubliners of a certain class small enough to allow news to circulate with great speed.

Again, it is typical of Molly's thought processes that she quickly reverses her opinion, with a colloquial 'still': though the streets might be dangerous, the early hours of the morning have their own charm. Then we change gear once more to follow her – as so often, it is only after reading a few words we realize that she has shifted subject: 'they', it turns out, are men, and Molly is once more thinking about the relationship between Bloom and Stephen. The logic of Molly's either/or is not impeccable, but the sense is clear enough: friendship is a problem because (a) men want sex from you and (b) other women are competitive and vicious. The passage ends with Molly's assertion that women deserve the bad treatment they get from men. This does not mean, however, that Molly has no feminist impulses; on the contrary, she is just as hard on men, and ready to celebrate women, when the mood takes her. What strikes one above all – and must have struck many readers, especially men, in the 1920s – is how little of Molly's rich inner life is guessed at by her husband and her lover.

In the final pages of the novel Molly's wandering thoughts combine memories of her girlhood in Gibraltar with a recollection of Bloom's proposal on Howth Head, and rise to a climax that manages to be both funny and moving, thanks to the way in which Molly's pragmatic reasoning ('I knew I could always get round him' [1580–81]; 'and I thought well as well him as another' [1604–5]) and calculated techniques of seduction ('the day I got him to propose to me' [1573–4]; 'drew him down to me so he could feel my breasts all perfume' [1607–8]) act as a foil to the romantic affirmation with which her monologue, and the book, closes: 'yes I said yes I will Yes.' The reader who reaches that final 'Yes' after the lengthy and tumultuous journey of the novel, with its satiric exposure of the pretensions and prejudices of modern culture, is likely to feel that this is Joyce's final affirmation, too, of a world of idiosyncrasy, imperfection and unfulfilment that is at the same time a world of small victories, genuine connections and generous laughter.

9

FINNEGANS WAKE I: THE PARENTS

Yoh! Brontolone slaaps yoh snoores. Upon Benn Heather, in
Seeple Isout too. The cranic head on him, caster of his reasons, peer yuthner in yondmist. Whooth? His clay feet,
swarded in verdigrass, stick up starck where he last fellonem,
by the mund of the magazine wall, where our maggy seen all,
with her sisterin shawl. While over against this belles' alliance
beyind III Sixty, ollollowed ill! bagsides of the fort, bom,
tarabom, tarabom, lurk the ombushes, the site of the lyffing-
in-wait of the upjock and hockums. Hence when the clouds
roll by, jamey, a proudseye view is enjoyable of our mounding's
mass, now Wallinstone national museum, with, in some green-
ish distance, the charmful waterloose country and the two
quitewhite villagettes who hear show of themselves so giggle-
somes minxt the follyages, the prettilees! Penetrators are
permitted into the museomound free.

Finnegans Wake I.1 (7.27–8.05)

First she let her hair fal and down it flussed to her feet its
teviots winding coils. Then, mothernaked, she sampood herself with galawater and fraguant pistania mud, wupper and
lauar, from crown to sole. Next she greased the groove of her
keel, warthes and wears and mole and itcher, with antifouling

butterscatch and turfentide and serpenthyme and with leaf-mould she ushered round prunella isles and eslats dun, quincecunct, allover her little mary. Peeld gold of waxwork her jellybelly and her grains of incense anguille bronze. And after that she wove a garland for her hair. She pleated it. She plaited it. Of meadowgrass and riverflags, the bulrush and waterweed, and of fallen griefs of weeping willow. Then she made her bracelets and her anklets and her armlets and a jetty amulet for necklace of clicking cobbles and pattering pebbles and rumble-down rubble, richmond and rehr, of Irish rhunerhinerstones and shellmarble bangles. That done, a dawk of smut to her airy ey, Annushka Lutetiavitch Pufflovah, and the lellipos cream to her lippeleens and the pick of the paintbox for her pommettes, from strawbirry reds to extra violates, and she sendred her boudeloire maids to His Affluence, Ciliegia Grande and Kirschie Real, the two chirsines, with respecks from his missus, seepy and sewery, and a request might she passe of him for a minnikin.

Finnegans Wake I.8 (206.29–207.14)

After the publication of *Ulysses* in 1922, Joyce became a literary hero – in spite (or perhaps partly because) of the fact that the book was banned in Britain and the USA and blocked by customs officials in Ireland.[14] Copies of the book were smuggled into English-speaking countries, and many of those who hadn't read it had at least heard of it. Given this success, Joyce might have been expected to carry on writing in the same vein, aiming to bring out a second *Ulysses* in a few years to cement his reputation and increase his earnings. But he wasn't really writing in a 'vein' when he finished *Ulysses*: each of the later episodes involved a new approach to fictional style and structure. If he had published, say, 'Circe', 'Eumaeus', 'Ithaca' and 'Penelope' as separate volumes, he would be known as the author of four very different books. So *Finnegans Wake*'s revolutionary approach to language and structure was in fact a development of what he had begun earlier in the verbal experimentation of parts of *Ulysses*. (*Dubliners* and *A Portrait of the Artist* can be thought of as the first stages in this ceaseless search for fresh ways of representing human experience and human history in language.)

Having moved to Paris in 1920 on Pound's suggestion, he and his family (his partner Nora, his son Giorgio, and his daughter Lucia) stayed there for nineteen years. Joyce's literary celebrity grew but his financial situation – in spite of the support of generous benefactors and increasing income from his writing – remained precarious, and the family moved their residence some eighteen times during this period. No doubt he hoped to finish the new book in a few years (*Ulysses* had taken eight), but the scale of the project together with his own difficulties, notably increasing blindness and the need to care for a schizophrenic daughter, meant that the work begun in 1922 was not published until 1939, on the eve of a world war, just as *Dubliners* and the serialized *Portrait* had been. However, the literary community had been given several glimpses of his 'work in progress' – he kept its title a secret until publication day – in magazines and small volumes. As well as introducing a new kind of literary language, the completed work was a challenging 628 pages long, again without section or chapter titles. Not surprisingly, it cemented Joyce's reputation as a 'difficult' writer, and remains for many who have heard about it or dipped into it the most forbidding of all literary works.

Yet it has provided entertainment and enlightenment to thousands of readers, by no means all of them scholars or academics. Once again, it is a matter of expectations. Very few people have the time or the financial support to enable them to read the entire book with the attention to detail that every page, every sentence, demands – and even those few who have done so admit that many words and phrases remain obscure. So there is no point in expecting meaning to leap from the page as it does with most reading material; and it would be even more unwise than it is with *Ulysses* to expect the language to be entirely at the service of a plot and a group of characters. If in reading *Ulysses* one has to skip many inscrutable terms or phrases to enjoy the onward momentum of the work, knowing that one will be able to look them up afterwards, the same is even truer of *Finnegans Wake* – except that there is no guarantee that one will ever find the answer in a reference book or annotation. At the same time, there are even more riches on every page, so that one can miss a significant proportion of the possible meanings and still get one's teeth into a great deal. And since plot has become secondary to the multiplication of meaning in every line, there is little danger of overlooking a crucial piece of information or twist in the action.

Finnegans Wake is a book of comedy, to a greater extent even than *Ulysses*. Its humour lies primarily in its play with language – the universal humour of distortion and double meaning, patterning and nonsense that made us laugh as young children and continues to amuse all but the most strait-laced of adults. Just as *Ulysses* made fun of the pretensions of heroic legend and the ideology that it serves, so the *Wake* punctures the images of white male superiority that underwrite militarism and colonialism abroad and patriarchal domination at home. All kinds of rhetorical self-importance are mocked, including the scholarly analysis of manuscripts, the sage chronicling of historical events, the blaring advertisement, the pompous lecture and the hypocritical sermon. The book relies on sound more than most works of fiction, and a puzzling passage may become hilariously clear if read aloud. It also benefits immensely from being read in a group: different members of the group will notice different meanings, and pooled insights can generate further understanding. (And the book often seems even funnier when it is being read collaboratively.) Like *Ulysses*, one way in which it provides pleasure is by means of repetition and recognition, since it is all the more satisfying to recognize a familiar motif when there is so much to baffle and bemuse.

Joyce's major innovation, introduced in a few places in *Ulysses* but made into the building-block of *Finnegans Wake*, is the portmanteau word (a term coined by Lewis Carroll, whose Humpty Dumpty explained to Alice that it suggests 'two meanings packed up into one word'). Let's take one phrase in the first passage above: 'proudseye view'. Reading this aloud, you are quite likely to hear 'bird's-eye view', and your first instinct may well be to 'translate' Joyce's odd phrase into this normal one. But the point about the portmanteau is that it combines two (or often more) meanings, and they operate *simultaneously*, so we don't leave 'proudseye' behind in jumping to the regularized version: the view is one to make the onlooker proud, as well as one from a vertical height. The portmanteau is like a pun (and there are many of these in the *Wake* as well), with the difference that it opens up the language to multiple possibilities, not just two.

This innovation, together with the fusing of plot lines, characters, places, times, tones and languages made possible by it, proved a hard morsel for the public to swallow. For forty or fifty years after its publication, *Finnegans Wake* tended to be the preserve of specialists – including a surprisingly large number of non-academics who found themselves captivated by it – and many Joyce scholars simply ignored it. The picture has now changed and, although few would claim to know the work intimately in the way that one can know Joyce's other books, an appreciation of the *Wake*'s achievement as well as its problematic challenge to the processes of reading are an integral part of most studies of Joyce. In recent years, Joyce's procedures in writing the book have become clearer, and scholars studying his notebooks and drafts have begun to track down the vast quantity of source materials from which he copied thousands of short phrases to weave into his polysemic palimpsest.

Although there is much to be gained from reading *Finnegans Wake* from cover to cover as if it were a normal novel, the full wealth of what the book has to offer can only come from spending the time on a single short passage one might usually spend on reading a chapter. What this means is that for most of us, given that there are other things we want to do with our lives besides immerse ourselves in Joyce's last work, the best compromise is to read through once without pausing too long to puzzle out details (one of many available outlines of the book will help in doing this) and then to select individual chapters or passages to devote more attention to. If time won't allow both of these modes of reading, there is more to be gained from adopting the latter strategy and relying on summaries to get a sense of what the rest of the book is like. Because there is very little plot in the usual sense of the word, it is not essential to read the chapters in sequence, and although it is a pity to miss any of Joyce's extraordinary writing, leaving out one or more chapters will not prove a great drawback in reading the others.

In approaching a passage of the *Wake* (and let's imagine for the moment that we have no knowledge of the rest of the book), it is best not to try *too* hard at first: a read-through, preferably aloud, will usually make the syntactic structure clear (Joyce tended to stay within the norms of sentence construction) and disclose some aspects of the theme. In our first passage, the syntax is not difficult, and we quickly gain a sense of a sleeping, snoring figure, whose feet are sticking up. There is a lot of battle imagery, although this gives way to what sounds like girlish laughter. We end with what could be a sign on a museum. In trying to make sense of the passage above, different readers will spot different portmanteau words and phrases. Most of us will hear 'upjock and hockums' as a weird variant of 'up, Guards, and at 'em!', though we might have to ruminate a bit longer over the transformation undergone by this familiar phrase, attributed to Wellington at the Battle of Waterloo. Once we have made this connection, we will hear 'Wallinstone' as 'Wellington', while the references to 'stone' and 'wall' (which some readers will link to another famous General) will cross-fertilize with 'mound' (in 'mud', 'moundings's' and 'museomound'), 'mass' and 'museum' to suggest a substantial building of some kind. The 'two quitewhite villagettes' could be two villages on the battlefield. It is obvious that 'Waterloo' is in 'waterloose', though there appears to be a loosing of waters as well. In a typical transhistorical leap, a Napoleonic battle is fused with a much later one in 'Ill Sixty, ollollowed ill': Hill 60, near Ypres, was fiercely fought over during the Second World War and is indeed hallowed by the many deaths that occurred on it.

Some readers will know a little more about the battle of Waterloo, or will look it up. (The Internet almost seems to have been invented to assist in understanding the *Wake*.) For instance, the battle is best known on the Continent by the name of a village on the site, La Belle Alliance – hence 'belles' alliance'. Others will be familiar with Dublin geography (something which is of as much value in reading the *Wake* as it is in reading *Ulysses*), and will recognize a number of distorted names. The River Liffey is obvious in 'lyffing', and the Hill of Howth, which projects out from the mainland on one side of Dublin Bay, is referred to twice, first as Benn Heather (its Irish name is Binn Éadair, and it has heather growing on it) and then as the question 'Whooth?' (As we have seen, Howth is a significant place in *Ulysses*, too, since it was where Molly accepted Bloom.) 'Seeple Isout' is just distinguishable (again more by the ear than the eye) as Chapelizod, a village on the Liffey next to Phoenix Park, in the western part of the city. (Does 'Isout' also name, as two words, the state of the sleeping figure?) The 'magazine wall' – echoed in 'maggy seen all' – is another Phoenix Park feature, the Magazine Fort being the munitions storehouse for the Dublin garrison; and so is the Wellington Monument – a tall obelisk in the park – which is here transformed into a museum.

What is emerging is the misty, gigantic figure of a man lying stretched across Dublin, his head on (or as) the Hill of Howth (its castle is alluded to in 'caster'), his feet in Phoenix Park. He is called 'Brontolone' in this passage (though this will turn out to be one of hundreds of names he receives), which an Italian speaker might recognize as meaning 'grumbler' – Joyce's portmanteaus are by no means restricted to English – but might also suggest the hugeness of a brontosaurus and the loudness of thunder (from Greek, *brontē*). He seems to be in some danger of being ambushed, however, and of being on display as if in a museum.

Let us now imagine coming to this passage with a little more knowledge of the themes, motifs and characters of the *Wake*, gained from reading other passages or from introductions to the work. There appear throughout the book a number of older male figures – heroes, generals, politicians, fathers, husbands – all of whom have suffered some kind of fall, and all of whom coalesce in the major male presence, most commonly known only by the initials HCE. Joyce may have taken these initials from the nineteenth-century statesman H. C. E. Childers, known because of his girth as 'Here Comes Everybody'; they recur in names and phrases on many pages, but if there is one that is more fundamental than the others it is 'Humphrey Chimpden Earwicker'. Joyce combed encyclopaedias, newspapers, history books and a host of other writings for examples of masculine pretension and collapse, heroic and trivial, ancient and recent, and the character of HCE – or perhaps a better term would be the HCE principle – unites all of these.

In our passage HCE is manifested as the giant in the Dublin
landscape; other avatars include Humpty Dumpty, Parnell,
Noah, Adam, Ibsen's master builder, and Roderick O'Connor,
the last king of Ireland. More generally, he is any hill, mountain, mound (as in 'mund' and 'mounding's mass'), or –
remembering the Hill of Howth – any castle or, by extension,
any city (and more particularly, of course, the city of Dublin).
In his most quotidian existence he is a publican who runs a
pub in Chapelizod, and his 'fall' involves an incident in nearby
Phoenix Park involving two girls and three soldiers. The story
of this disgrace takes a host of forms, but at its most innocuous
it entails voyeurism on the part of HCE, who watches the two
girls peeing behind some bushes, and is seen in turn by the
three soldiers – who then spread the story of his transgression
around the city. There are more incriminating versions of
HCE's sin, though nothing worse than exhibitionism seems to
be involved.

Familiarity with this narrative and its centrality in the *Wake*
illuminates the passage greatly. The giant – HCE in one of his
guises – is a fallen figure who has proved to have feet of clay,
figuratively at least, since 'verdigrass' suggests the verdigris
that covers exposed copper. 'Verdigrass' also implies the green
grass of the park where the giant's feet 'stick up starck', and
'swarded' carries connotations of both 'sward', to remind us of
the grass again, and 'swathed'. The feet stick up 'where he last
fellonem', or fell on them, which is also where 'our maggy
seen all, with her sisterin shawl'. In other words, his fall was
observed by two sisters, one of whom is called 'Maggy' and
the other of whom was wearing a shawl – though if we
remember the occurrence of the word 'shawl' in the 'Cyclops'
episode of *Ulysses* we will know that it can also mean 'prostitute'. In this version of the tale HCE seems to do more than
simply spy on the girls, since the girls have 'seen all' – it is presumably not only his feet that 'stick up starck'. We can't ignore

the phallic shape of the Wellington Monument either, and the 'proudseye view' of 'our mounding's mass' is another indication of the part of HCE's anatomy the sisters saw – standing proud and, as Molly says in 'Penelope', 'with a kind of eye in it' (18.816). Lurking and lying in wait in ambush behind the fort, however, are the soldiers, signalled by military music in 'bom, tarabom, tarabom' and by the echo of Wellington's command to his men. The two girls clearly also constitute the 'belles' alliance' and 'the two quitewhite villagettes', and by the end of the passage it is they who are committing the folly of exposing themselves in the bushes (hence 'follyages'), giggling as they pee. (We now appreciate the second meaning of 'waterloose'; and 'minxt' suggests not only minxes but Latin *minxit*, she urinated.) As the passage ends, we are encouraged to visit the museum – and what follows this passage is in fact a guided tour, in which the battle of Waterloo, and energetic sexual encounters, receive further attention.

This commentary is by no means exhaustive. Consultation of annotations will reveal further allusions that few readers would have picked up without aid: how many of us are familiar with the song 'Wait till the clouds roll by, Jenny'? Or would associate the word 'clouds' with the Pont de St Cloud over the Seine? (The latter interpretation will seem far-fetched until it is pointed out that in the space of ten pages Joyce weaves in the names of twenty-four Paris bridges; another one in this passage is the Pont National.) Furthermore, there are many riddles remaining: why does Wellington's phrase become 'upjock and hockum'? Why does 'Jenny' become 'Jamey'? (A sly reference to the author?) What's important to remember is that the passage can come to life with a remarkable complexity of meaning even with many of its elements unaccounted for. And there is always the possibility of a penny suddenly dropping, and another sparkle of sense flashing out.

But what is really happening in this passage? the reader may ask. One answer is that several things are happening at once, and that Joyce has fused them to highlight similarities and differences: a tourist guide is pointing out some features of the Dublin landscape, Wellington is engaged in battle with Napoleon, and three soldiers are watching an older man spying on, or exposing himself to, two girls in the bushes. None of these is the 'primary' or 'literal' level; the portmanteau technique serves to blend them so thoroughly that no hierarchy emerges. Another answer is that it is not a book premised on a sequence (or even constellation) of events at all, but rather that it is a gigantic series of parodies and spoofs of different ways of writing and speaking about the world, about history, about relationships, about sex, about religion, and a multitude of other topics. In this passage we can hear and see the bardic poet, the tour guide, the military historian, the purveyor of soft porn, and the sign-writer, all sounding together in a polyphonic weave.

The second passage describes the major female figure in *Finnegans Wake* – the wife of HCE, the mother of their three children, but also a river, any river but especially the River Liffey as it flows from the Wicklow Hills through Dublin to the sea. Her name in the passage is given as Annushka Lutetiavitch Pufflovah, but this is only one of hundreds of versions: what remains consistent are her initials, the most usual expansion of which is Anna Livia Plurabelle. The reason for the elaborate self-beautification, which readers familiar with the *Iliad* will recognize as a rewriting of the passage in Book XIV in which Juno prepares herself to captivate Zeus, is that she has decided to venture forth in defence of HCE's reputation after the story of his misdemeanour has spread far and wide. The parts of the female body and the attributes of the river are intermingled as she washes herself, upper and lower

(or 'wupper and lauar'), then anoints those lower regions
before attending to her hair, her jewellery and finally make-up
for her eyes, lips and cheeks. She then sends her two maids –
and two girls in the *Wake*, whoever else they are, are always
also the two girls in the park, here both with names that
mean 'cherry' – to HCE ('His Affluence') to request that she
might be allowed a minute to relieve herself. ('Minnikin' is
both 'minute' and a reference to the famous Brussels statue
of a boy urinating.) This, of course, is a ploy to enable her
to escape and carry out her plan, which, it turns out, consists
of distributing gifts – not all of them pleasant – to all her
husband's detractors; or, in riverine terms, to spread flotsam
on the banks by flooding.

Once again, there are many portmanteaus that build on
Irish place names: the names of ALP's boudoir maids, 'Ciliegia
Grande and Kirschie Real', for instance, appropriately suggest
the two canals that run to the north and south of the Liffey in
Dublin, the Grand Canal and the Royal Canal. Others build
on the words of a song ('richmond and rehr' refers us to
Thomas Moore's 'Rich and Rare Were the Gems she Wore',
an appropriate song in this context) and words in other languages (*prunelle* and *pommettes*, French for pupil of the eye and
cheekbones). The majority, however, fuse a word being used
in the description of ALP with the name of a river. Just as the
'Lestrygonians' chapter of *Ulysses* throws up words associated
with food and eating, so this chapter of *Finnegans Wake*, which
is all about Anna Livia, is thronged with river names. This
passage alone contains about thirty-five, most of which would
be unknown to the average reader (though it is always possible that the river in your own neighbourhood, of no renown
at all, will pop out at you). British readers will notice the
Teviot (made to sound like 'devious'), the Wear (associated
with the river's weirs), the Itchen ('itcher' is slang for vagina),
and – lakes are allowed in as well – the Serpentine (combined

with both thyme and, matching 'tide' in 'turfentide', time); also easily recognizable are the Rhine (combined with rhine-stones in 'rhunerrhinerstones') and the Loire (helping to create 'boudeloire'). And in the phrase 'missus, seepy and sewery' – suggesting ALP's, and the Liffey's, occasional slug-gishness and smell – we hear the names of two famous American rivers.

As in *Ulysses*, and especially its final episode, Joyce makes use of gender stereotypes: HCE is the upright structure, ALP the flowing and changing river; HCE is the sexual predator (however ineffective his assault), ALP the forgiving and sup-portive partner. Yet in this work, too, stereotypes are the material which Joyce exploits for comic and critical purposes, not ideological blinkers he adopts. HCE's manliness is always being subjected to downfall and humiliation, while ALP is often the more active and adventurous figure. Sex is central to the book, as both that which causes the fall and that which redeems it: the edifices of culture (largely patriarchal) are brought down by the stirrings of desire; but desire in turn produces regeneration and generosity.

The excess of river names in this chapter offers a clear demonstration that it is not crucial to get every allusion or catch every double meaning in the *Wake*: to know a few of the rivers named here is quite enough to enjoy Joyce's verbal and geographical tapestry – and there's a particular delight in knowing that different readers will find different rivers. It is far from a truism that every reader makes *Finnegans Wake* their own.

10

FINNEGANS WAKE II: THE CHILDREN

Who sleeps in now number one, for example? A pussy, purr esimple. Cunina, Statulina and Edulia, but how sweet of her! Has your pussy a pessname? Yes, indeed, you will hear it passim in all the noveletta and she is named Buttercup. Her bare name will tellt it, a monitress. How very sweet of her and what an excessively lovecharming missyname to forsake, now that I come to drink of it filtred, a gracecup fulled of bitterness. She is dadad's lottiest daughterpearl and brooder's cissiest auntybride.

* * *

Would one but to do apart a lilybit her virginelles and, so, to breath, so, therebetween, behold, she had instantt with her handmade as to graps the myth inmid the air. Mother of moth! I will to show herword in flesh. Approach not for ghost sake! It is dormition! She may think, what though little doth she realise, as morning fresheth, it hath happened her, you know what, as they too what two dare not utter. Silvoo plush, if scolded she draws a face. Petticoat's asleep but in the gentlenest of her thoughts apoo is a nursepin. To be presented, Babs for Bimbushi? Of courts and with enticers. Up, girls, and at him!

Finnegans Wake III.4 (561.08–16, 24–33)

And since we are talking amnessly of brukasloop crazedledaze, who doez in sleeproom number twobis? The twobirds. Holy policeman, O, I see! Of what age are your birdies? They are to come of twinning age so soon as they may be born to be eldering like those olders while they are living under chairs. They are and they seem to be so tightly tattached as two maggots to touch other, I think I notice, do I not? You do. Our bright bull babe Frank Kevin is on heartsleeveside. Do not you waken him! Our farheard bode. He is happily to sleep, limb of the Lord, with his lifted in blessing, his buchel losa, like the blissed angel he looks so like and his mou is semiope as though he were blowdelling on a bugigle.

* * *

Hush! The other, twined on codliverside, has been crying in his sleep, making sharpshape his inscissors, on some first choice sweets fished out of the muck. A stake in our mead. What a teething wretch! How his book of craven images! Here are posthumious tears on his intimelle. And he has pipettishly bespilled himself from his foundingpen as illspent from inkinghorn. He is jem job joy pip poo pat (jot um for a sobrat!) Jerry Jehu. You will know him by name in the capers but you cannot see whose heel he sheepfolds in his wrought hand because I have not told it to you. O, foetal sleep! Ah, fatal slip!

Finnegans Wake III.4 (562.16–27; 563.1–10)

Finnegans Wake is divided into four books, all but the last further subdivided into chapters – the first book into eight, the next two into four. Each chapter is distinctive, not so much in basic style – they all use the portmanteau consistently – but in structure and theme. A large part of the first book is introductory: we are given a number of manifestations of a fall, from the sleeping giant in the Dublin landscape (identified with the Irish mythic hero, Finn MacCool, whose

name is included in the book's title) to the builder Tim
Finnegan, who falls from a ladder while laying bricks in a wall
and is assumed to be dead, but is resurrected at his wake after
being splashed with whiskey. The phrase 'Finnegan's wake'
most obviously refers to this story – enshrined in a popular
ballad Joyce heard in Dublin – although the omission of an
apostrophe opens up various other meanings, including the
suggestion that the Finnegans (the Irish, perhaps?) are waking
up. All these falls are connected to one another (often
through portmanteau words) and, at the two extremes of significance, to the Fall of Man and to HCE's peccadillo in
Phoenix Park.

We also learn in Book I of a letter found in a rubbish
dump by a hen, an avatar of ALP; and this letter is to reappear
in different guises throughout the book. We hear of invasions
(HCE, it seems, is himself a foreigner in Dublin, reminding us
of Bloom), wars, a kidnapping (derived from a historical event
that took place at Howth Castle), and a love story based on
the legend of Tristan and Isolde (Chapelizod is, by etymology,
the chapel of Isolde; the cuckolded King Mark is another
fallen hero). From the end of first chapter through the next
three we are given the story of HCE, including another version of 'the sin in the park' (which this time involves a
homosexual encounter), the gossip that follows, a trial, and
flight. All the time, of course, Joyce's portmanteau style and
freedom from normal narrative constraints allows him to make
connections among a multitude of people, places and stories,
historical and fictional.

The following chapters of Book I provide further insights
into the other major characters, who form a nuclear family:
apart from the parents HCE and ALP, there are twin sons,
most often known as Shem and Shaun, and a younger daughter called Issy. Various other characters are introduced, notably
four old men who chronicle the history of Ireland (and the

sexual activities of the other characters), twelve adult Dubliners who appear on public occasions, and twenty-eight girls – the 'rainbow girls' or the 'maggies' – who often accompany Issy, and sometimes appear to be multiplied versions of her. Shem and Shaun are totally different types: the first is an artist (or a would-be artist), impractical, slovenly, outcast, but with a certain charm and perhaps some genuine creativity; the second is practical, materialistic, successful and self-satisfied. The former, it seems, is responsible for writing ALP's letter, the latter, in his guise as postman, for distributing it. They are constantly at odds with one another, though together they constitute a threat to their father as they combine to displace him – their combination often spawning a third male figure, resulting in a trio we recognize as the three soldiers. Issy represents the temptation to older males of young female sexuality, and as she is often encountered in conversation with her mirror-image, she is linked through this doubling to the two girls in the park. HCE's indiscretion with the girls, whatever it was, thus acquires a whiff of incest. She, too, threatens to displace her mother, who is aware that her sexual attraction is diminishing while Issy's is at its peak.

At the end of Book I chapter 8, darkness is falling, and the following two books are set largely at night. Joyce called *Finnegans Wake* a 'nightbook' in contrast to *Ulysses*, although much of *Ulysses* occurs at night, and much of *Finnegans Wake* has no particular nocturnal connection. More significant is the link between the distortions of language in the *Wake* and those that occur in dreams, notably condensation, the fusion of two ideas into one image or word, and displacement, or the shifting of emphasis from what is truly important to what is apparently trivial. For Freud, these distortions signalled the operations of the unconscious, but this does not mean *Finnegans Wake* is an attempt to make the unconscious speak. Joyce's meticulous, labour-intensive creative process is as far from the automatic writing that fascinated Yeats and many others as could be imagined.

The first two chapters of Book 2 deal with the children's world: they play games at evening (Shem vying with Shaun for the attention of Issy and the maggies) before being hustled inside, and there they do their homework, which can also be read as an investigation of their mother's genitalia as the source of their own being. Chapter 3 of Book II returns to HCE, now as publican, and elaborates on a story in which an Irish soldier fails to kill a Russian general with his pants down; and chapter 4 recounts the love-making of Tristan and Isolde, only barely recognizable as the characters of medieval legend and Wagnerian opera, as witnessed by the four old men. The first three chapters of Book III focus attention on Shaun, who goes through successive transformations as he is publicly interviewed, delivers a long and hypocritical lecture to Issy (full of sexual suggestiveness), and is interrogated by the four old men. Towards the end of Book III chapter 4, HCE reappears, offering a spirited defence of his actions. In the fourth chapter – from which the passage above is taken – we visit the central family in their domestic incarnation as the Porters. Finally, the single chapter that makes up Book IV announces dawn, revisits HCE's sin, stages a dispute between St Patrick – another invader of Ireland – and a native Druid, provides a final version of the letter, and ends with a moving soliloquy from ALP as the River Liffey flowing into the sea.

By the time we reach the passage above we have encountered the siblings Shaun, Shem and Issy in a myriad of guises, at a variety of ages, and under a host of names. Now, in the final chapter of Book III, we come upon one of the most intimate renderings of their differing personalities: as sleeping children. We are in the company of an enquiring visitor being shown the upper floors of the pub in which the Porter family are in their beds. Without making sense of it all, the reader will immediately take from the first passage an aura of childishness and innocence. The language exudes a saccharine tenderness: 'How sweet of her!'; 'How very sweet of her and what an excessively lovecharming missyname'. (Although she is now called 'Buttercup', the name 'Issy' is concealed in 'missyname', or maiden name.) Issy is a purring cat, she is adored by her father, her dearest friend is her reflection in the mirror. She makes a face if she is scolded, but she is now asleep – 'pussycat' conceals 'petticoat' – and her thoughts form a gentle nest. The words themselves are sometimes childish: 'dadad's', 'lilybit', 'Silvoo plush' (instead of 's'il vous plaît'), 'apoo'. Joyce is clearly parodying the sentimentalized speech often used to and about children, especially girls.

We know, however, that Issy does not stand for innocence in the book; rather, the appearance of innocence is part of her sexual appeal (a combination that is one of the *Wake*'s more disturbing implications). If she is a 'pussy' it is unlikely that the word refers only to cats. 'Lovecharming' may at first sight seem innocuous, but in the context of Issy's legendary counterpart Isolde, it conjures up the love charm or philtre ('to drink of it filtred') that produced the fatal passion between the two heroic lovers – truly a 'gracecup fulled with bitterness'. The affection her father feels for her ('dadad's lottiest daughterpearl') is tainted by the reference to Lot, who fathered children on his daughters. We return to Tristan and Isolde in the next phrase ('brooder's cissiest auntybride'), since Isolde, as the wife of Tristan's uncle Mark, is his aunt. And what are we to make of the action that the speaker undertakes, as he or she moves to 'do apart a lilybit her virginelles'? Perhaps it is the bedclothes that need to be opened up a little to reveal the girl, as she makes a gesture with her hand as if to grasp a moth in the air. But the association of 'lily' with purity, followed by 'virgin', suggests a different part of the anatomy; is the 'myth' perhaps the one that tells of Cupid's passion for Psyche, the young girl who was not allowed to see the god who was pleasuring her each night? (The word 'psyche' can mean 'moth', after all.) But if so, it is only a dream, and Issy's pleasure is in fact derived from the action of her hand ('inmid the air' could suggest pubic hair) – a vivid dream, however, as we are told in stumbling language that she might think she has lost her virginity during the night.

There is another register the reader may notice, one that may seem far removed from either childish innocence or sexual precocity: religion. If we do some research we discover that the exclamation 'Cunina, Statulina and Edulia' invokes three Roman goddesses connected with the upbringing of children. But it is the Christian imagery that is particularly telling. Mary is the handmaid ('handmade') of the Lord and the mother of God ('Mother of moth'); Jesus is the word made flesh ('herword in flesh'); the 'dormition' of the Virgin is the sleep that came upon her in lieu of death; and as a girl Mary was, according to the Apocrypha, 'presented' in the Temple, the subject of many paintings. This is not the first time Joyce has fused the adoration of the Virgin with the erotic appeal of young girls: in the 'Nausicaa' episode of *Ulysses*, Bloom's masturbation in response to Gerty's exhibitionism is intercut with the singing of a litany in the Virgin's honour. The threads are woven even more tightly here, thanks to the synthesis of meaning made possible by Joyce's verbal technique. We are not invited to consider rationally the links between the worship of the Virgin, female sexual attractiveness, and girlish innocence, but to experience them simultaneously as a comic composition – though perhaps one with its dark side.

The passage ends with a phrase that echoes one in our previous example: 'Up, girls, and at him!' Wellington's supposed exhortation has occurred, in a variety of disguises, many times between these two instances, which are the first and the last in the book:[15] here, the phrase suggests (with an allusion to the girls in the park) female predators and a male victim. There are a large number of such repeated motifs in the *Wake*, often in distorted forms recognizable only because we have become accustomed to them, and more particularly to their rhythmic patterning. Variants of the Wellington phrase include 'upjump and pumpim' (10.16), 'Upwap and dump em' (18.36), 'uprip and jack him!' (179.08), 'Nip up and nab it!' (187.13), and 'Upanishadem!' (303.13). Like the repeated motifs in *Ulysses*, they help to bind the work in spite of its length and complexity, and provide pleasurable gleams of familiarity among the tangled thickets of prose.

The twins are sleeping in the other bedroom, and again we quickly reach a basic understanding of the scene. They are in the same bed, their bodies touching. The first is Kevin, Shaun's name in this domestic arena; he is the angelic twin, 'bright', fair-haired ('farheard' – he is clearly loud as well), sleeping happily with his mouth half-open as if he were blowing on a bugle (though he might be pedalling on a bicycle). Some research into the puzzling phrase 'buchel Iosa' complicates the picture slightly, as it turns out that this is a reference to the staff of St Patrick, the Bachall Íosa, supposedly inherited from Jesus himself, combined with the Irish word 'buachaill', 'boy'. If his boy-staff is lifted in his sleep it seems likely that his dreams are not entirely innocent (and we have noted that there is evidence earlier in the book to suggest that Shaun's professions of purity and piety are hypocritical). The phrase used elsewhere for Shaun's staff might be appropriate here too: 'jewelled pederect' (155.23).

By contrast, Jerry – Shem – has been crying and chewing on some dirty sweets, and has spilled ink on himself from his fountain pen, as you might from a pipette or an inkhorn. Or, more likely, he has wet the bed with urine or semen; the portmanteau 'foundingpen' might suggest the procreative function of his penis rather than its urinary function. (Elsewhere 'Jerry' becomes 'Jerkoff' [563.24].) No wonder he is a 'stake in our mead' (another phallic image), as well as being a snake in our midst, a teething and teasing wretch, a worshipper of graven and fearful images. He has already had his name in the papers, no doubt because of some scandal or other; and 'capers' also suggests goats, by contrast with the sheep, whose side Kevin/Shaun is clearly on. Some Biblical knowledge helps here: when the birth of Esau and Jacob is described in Genesis, we are told that, after a struggle in the womb, Esau came out first, and then Jacob, his hand on Esau's heel. The identification of Esau – the older, upright twin – with Shaun, and Jacob – the younger, devious twin – with Shem is by this point in the book well established. It might seem odd that Kevin, identified with the sheep at the Last Judgement, should be sleeping on the 'heartsleeveside' or left side of the bed, and Jerry, identified with the goats, should be on the 'codliverside' or right. But if we think of paintings of Christ in judgement, the blessed – on Christ's right hand – are to be seen on the left, and the sinners are on the right. Since he is on the right-hand side of the bed as we look at it, Jerry, lying on his back, is able to hold Kevin's heel in his right hand, though 'wrought' suggests that, as so often, he is in the wrong in doing so.

The final phrases of the passage relate the happiness of sleep in the womb to a 'fatal slip', the fall that is repeated endlessly through Finnegans Wake. The paradox of a fall that is not simply to be condemned derives from St Augustine's doctrine of the Fall of Man as a felix culpa, a happy fault, in that it precipitated the coming of the Redeemer. Augustine's 'O felix culpa!' occurs repeatedly throughout the Wake, though of course one has to have one's ears well open to hear it. Some examples: 'O foenix culprit!' (23.16); 'O'Phelim's Cutprice'

(72.04); '*Ophelia's Culpreints*' (105.18); 'O'Faynix Coalprince' (139.35); 'O felicitous culpability' (263.29); 'phoenix his calipers' (332.31); 'fellows culpows' (363.20); 'Fu Li's gulpa' (426.17); 'O foolish coupled!' (433.30); 'Oh Finlay's cold-palled!' (506.09); 'Poor Feliz Culapert!' (536.08); 'O, felicious coolpose!' (618.01). That this phrase is repeated so often is not by chance: at the heart of *Finnegans Wake*'s exorbitant tour through the world's histories, languages, cultures and stories, and its comic exposure of human foolishness and pomposity, lies Joyce's growing conviction – not to be found in the more sardonic ironies of *Dubliners* or *A Portrait* but already becoming evident in the worldly tolerance of *Ulysses* – that the manifold imperfections and follies of our existence on earth are not, in the end, to be regretted and bemoaned, but celebrated as the source of the indispensable values of generosity, creativity and laughter. The shift from Stephen Dedalus's bitter evaluation of Ireland's narrowness to Leopold Bloom's acceptance of the limitations of Dublin life is taken further in the *Wake*, where the targets of mockery – which have remained much the same over Joyce's career – prove to be at the same time a fount of hilarity and high spirits.

In order to cram into his six-hundred-odd pages as many as possible of the world's cultural artefacts, historical records, imaginative creations and hidden desires Joyce found he had to invent a new language and a new literary form. The work has spawned many imitations, and encouraged writers to take similar risks, but it remains unsurpassed in the magnitude of its ambitions. For most new readers, a few chapters – or perhaps only a few passages – will be enough to experience the unique mixture of bafflement and pleasure that the book has to offer; but for some, it will become a store of entertaining comedy, intriguing puzzles, and occasional breathtaking beauty, to be dipped into for the rest of their lives.

NOTES

1 Margaret Anderson, *My Thirty Years' War* (1930), New York: Horizon Press, 1969, pp. 212–13. Paul Vanderham quotes part of this letter in his book *James Joyce and Censorship: The Trials of 'Ulysses'*, a study of the obscenity trials Joyce's novel faced between 1920 and 1934. He includes a useful appendix of all the passages deemed by one or more authorities to be obscene.

2 S. H. C., 'Ulysses', *The Carnegie Magazine* vii, No. 2 (Feb. 1934), 279–81; excerpted in Robert H. Deming, ed., *James Joyce: The Critical Heritage*, Routledge & Kegan Paul, 1970, vol. 1, p. 243.

3 Quoted by Ulick O'Connor in 'James Joyce and Oliver St. John Gogarty: A Famous Friendship', *Texas Quarterly* iii (Summer 1960), p. 191; excerpted in Deming, *James Joyce: The Critical Heritage*, vol. 1, pp. 282–3.

4 Shane Leslie, review of *Ulysses*, *Quarterly Review* ccxxxviii (October 1922), 219–34; excerpted in Deming, *James Joyce: The Critical Heritage*, vol. 1, p. 207.

5 *The Letters of James Joyce*, vol. 1, ed. Stuart Gilbert, New York: Viking, 1957, p. 275.

6 An excellent, accessible study of this aspect of the stories is Margot Norris, *Suspicious Readings of Joyce's 'Dubliners'*, Philadelphia: University of Pennsylvania Press, 2003.

7 See Don Gifford, *Joyce Annotated: Notes for 'Dubliners' and 'A Portrait of the Artist as a Young Man'*, 2nd edn, Berkeley: University of California Press, 1982, p. 219. The phrase comes from Hugh Miller, *The Testimony of the Rocks* (1857). That Stephen is not making up beautiful phrases but culling them from unlikely places in his reading hints at a creative process more like Joyce's in his later work and less like the contemporaries he seems to be imitating, though Joyce could not have expected his readers to pick this up.

8 No satisfactory source for this splendid phrase, which Joyce was fond of, has, to my knowledge, been found. Although it has been used in debates in the Irish parliament as if it were an established epithet, it is not certain that it pre-dates Joyce.

9 The last line was probably 'She pisses like a man'.
10 Did Joyce later learn that Samuel Beckett's ancestors, the Becquets, were Huguenot poplin manufacturers in eighteenth-century Dublin?
11 This is not strictly true, as there is a final full stop. Some editors also argue that Joyce intended a full stop halfway through.
12 Holbrook Jackson, review in *To-Day*, June 1922; excerpted in Deming, *James Joyce: The Critical Heritage*, vol. 1, pp. 199–200.
13 Sisley Huddleston, review in the *Observer*, March 1922; extract in Deming, *James Joyce: The Critical Heritage*, vol. 1, p. 216.
14 In a judgement that was a landmark in the history of censorship, Judge John M. Woolsey overturned the US ban on *Ulysses* in 1933, allowing American publication of the book by Random House in 1934. The first edition printed in Britain was the Bodley Head version, published in 1936.
15 Clive Hart, in *Structure and Motif in 'Finnegans Wake'*, Evanston: Northwestern University Press, 1962, gives 19 occurrences (p. 245) in his list of several hundred motifs.

CHRONOLOGY

1882 James Augustine Joyce born in Rathgar, Dublin, on 2 February, oldest surviving son of John Stanislaus Joyce, collector of rates, and Mary Jane ('May') Joyce (*née* Murray).

1884 Stanislaus Joyce, James's closest companion among his siblings, born.

1888 Enters Clongowes Wood College, an elite Jesuit school, aged 6, as boarder.

1891 First printed work, a verse broadside on the death of Parnell. Withdrawn from Clongowes.

1892 The Joyces leave the prosperous suburbs for a smaller house in the city; they will move several times in the years while Joyce remains in Ireland.

1893 Admitted free to Belvedere College, Dublin. John Joyce forced to sell his Cork properties to satisfy creditors.

1895 Elected to the Sodality of Our Lady.

1897 Wins academic prizes, including best English composition in Ireland.

1898 Enters University College, Dublin.

1900 Writes a play, now lost, entitled *A Brilliant Career*. Lectures on 'Drama and Life'; essay on 'Ibsen's New Drama' published. Begins writing 'epiphanies'.

1901 Writes and prints at his own expense pamphlet entitled 'The Day of the Rabblement'. Translates two plays by Gerhart Hauptmann.

1902 Essay on 'James Clarence Mangan' published. Graduates from the university and leaves Ireland for Paris, ostensibly to study medicine. Returns home for Christmas.

1903 Back in Paris for a short period; gives up the idea of studying medicine. Mother's illness takes him back to Dublin; she dies. Continues to write reviews.

1904 Begins *Stephen Hero* and writes first *Dubliners* stories, published in *The Irish Homestead*. Writes and publishes poems. Gets teaching job in Dalkey; spends six days in Sandycove Martello tower. Meets Nora Barnacle; four months later leaves Ireland with her. Takes up job as English teacher with Berlitz School, Pola (now in Croatia).

1905 Transferred to Berlitz School in Trieste. Submits manuscript of

Dubliners to Grant Richards, London publisher, who first accepts then declines it. Son Giorgio born. Stanislaus moves to Trieste.

1906 Moves to Rome to work in a bank; finds it frustrating. Begins work on 'The Dead'.

1907 Returns to Trieste. Publishes first collection of poems, *Chamber Music*. Writes articles in Italian for a Trieste newspaper. Completes 'The Dead' and begins transforming *Stephen Hero* into *A Portrait of the Artist as a Young Man*. Daughter Lucia born.

1908 Three chapters of *A Portrait of the Artist as a Young Man* completed.

1909 Travels to Ireland with Giorgio for a visit, signs contract for *Dubliners* with Maunsel & Co., Dublin publishers. Back in Trieste, gets business support to start first movie theatre in Ireland. Returns to Dublin, and opens Volta Cinema.

1910 Returns to Trieste. The Volta fails.

1912 Last visit to Ireland. Maunsel abandons *Dubliners*.

1914 Grant Richards agrees to publish *Dubliners*; it appears on 15 June. *A Portrait of the Artist as a Young Man* begins serial publication in *The Egoist* (London). Starts work on *Ulysses* and *Exiles*.

1915 Stanislaus interned for remainder of the war. *Exiles* completed. Permitted to leave Trieste for Switzerland; settles in Zurich. Receives money from the Royal Literary Fund, thanks to efforts of Pound, Yeats and Gosse.

1916 *A Portrait of the Artist as a Young Man* published by B. W. Huebsch (New York).

1917 *A Portrait* published by Egoist Press (London). First of many gifts from Harriet Shaw Weaver. First eye surgery.

1918 *The Little Review* (New York) begins to publish *Ulysses* in serial form. *Exiles* published in England and the United States.

1919 Joyce family returns to Trieste. Teaches English at a commercial school and works on *Ulysses*.

1920 Meets Pound in Italy; persuaded by Pound to move to Paris. *The Little Review* forced to abandon serial publication of *Ulysses* owing to court order.

1921 Final stages of *Ulysses*. Larbaud gives laudatory lecture.

1922 *Ulysses* published on 2 February, Joyce's birthday, by Shakespeare and Company, Paris bookshop. Nora and the children visit Ireland.

1923 First sketch for *Work in Progress* (*Finnegans Wake*) written.

1924 More severe eye trouble. First fragment of *Work in Progress* published in the *transatlantic review* (Paris).

1925 More sections of *Work in Progress* published.

1927 International protest against the piracy of *Ulysses* in USA. Several sections of *Finnegans Wake* published in *transition* (Paris) by Eugene Jolas. *Pomes Penyeach* published.

1928 *Anna Livia Plurabelle*, first of several sections of *Work in Progress* to be published in book form.

1929 French translation of *Ulysses* published. *Tales Told of Shem and Shaun* published. *Our Exagmination round His Factification for Incamination of Work in Progress* published.

1930 Series of eye operations in Zűrich. *Haveth Childers Everywhere* published.

1931 Marries Nora Barnacle in London 'for testamentary reasons.' John Stanislaus Joyce dies.

1932 Grandson, Stephen James Joyce, born. Lucia Joyce suffers mental breakdown.

1933 Judge John M. Woolsey rules that *Ulysses* is not pornographic. Lucia hospitalized.

1934 *Ulysses* published in New York. *The Mime of Mick, Nick and the Maggies* published.

1936 *Ulysses* published in London.

1937 *Storiella as She Is Syung* published.

1938 Completes *Finnegans Wake*.

1939 Advance copy of *Finnegans Wake* reaches Joyce on 2 February. Publication in London and New York. On the outbreak of war, leaves Paris for St Gérand-le-Puy, near Vichy.

1940 After occupation of France, family move to Zűrich, but forced to leave Lucia behind.

1941 Dies on 13 January, as a result of perforated ulcer. Buried in Fluntern cemetery, Zűrich.

1951 Nora Joyce dies in Zűrich.

SUGGESTIONS FOR FURTHER READING

The following is a highly selective list of accessible introductions, critical studies and reference works suitable for the reader developing an interest in Joyce. Many of these works contain suggestions for more advanced reading about Joyce and his historical, cultural and political context. See also 'A Note on Joyce's Texts' at the beginning of this book.

Introductions and Companions

General

Derek Attridge, ed. *The Cambridge Companion to Joyce*. Second edition. Cambridge: Cambridge University Press, 2004.

Richard Brown. *James Joyce: A Post-Culturalist Perspective*. London: Macmillan, 1992.

Eric Bulson. *The Cambridge Introduction to James Joyce*. Cambridge: Cambridge University Press, 2006.

Steven Connor. *James Joyce*. Plymouth: Northcote House, 1996.

Andrew Gibson, *James Joyce*. London: Reaktion Books, 2006. Particular emphasis on Joyce's political concerns.

Harry Levin. *James Joyce: A Critical Introduction* (1941). Revised edition. New York: New Directions Press, 1960. A pioneering but still valuable study.

Jean-Michel Rabaté, ed. *Palgrave Advances in James Joyce Studies*. Basingstoke: Palgrave Macmillan, 2004.

Reynolds, Mary T., ed. *James Joyce: A Collection of Critical Essays*. New York: Prentice-Hall, 1992.

Michael Seidel. *James Joyce: A Short Introduction*. Oxford: Blackwell, 2002.

Ulysses

Terence Killeen, *Ulysses Unbound: A Reader's Companion to James Joyce's 'Ulysses'*. Bray: Wicklow/National Library of Ireland, 2004. Informative chapter-by-chapter guide.

Margot Norris, ed. *A Companion to James Joyce's 'Ulysses'*. Boston: Bedford Books, 1998.

Vincent Sherry. *James Joyce: 'Ulysses'*. Cambridge: Cambridge University Press, 1994. Short introduction with helpful comments on historical context.

Finnegans Wake

Roland McHugh. *The 'Finnegans Wake' Experience*. Dublin: Irish Academic Press, 1981. The author's encounter with the *Wake*: a helpful way into the work.

Reference Works and Annotated Editions

General

A. Nicholas Fargnoli and Michael P. Gillespie. *James Joyce A–Z*. New York: Oxford University Press, 1995. A useful encyclopaedia.

Dubliners

Terence Brown, ed. *Dubliners*. London: Penguin, 1992. Useful introduction and notes.

Don Gifford. *Joyce Annotated: Notes for 'Dubliners' and 'A Portrait of the Artist as a Young Man'*. Second edition. Berkeley: University of California Press, 1982.

John Wyse Jackson and Bernard McGinley, eds. *James Joyce's 'Dubliners'*. London: Sinclair-Stevenson, 1993. Fully annotated and illustrated edition.

Jeri Johnson, ed. *Dubliners*. World's Classics. Oxford: Oxford University Press, 2000. Full introduction and notes.

Margot Norris, ed. *Dubliners: Norton Critical Edition*. New York: W. W. Norton, 2005. Includes valuable documentation and critical essays.

A Portrait of the Artist as a Young Man

Seamus Deane, ed. *A Portrait of the Artist as a Young Man*. London: Penguin, 1992. Useful introduction and notes.

Don Gifford. *Joyce Annotated: Notes for 'Dubliners' and 'A Portrait of the Artist as a Young Man'*. Second edition. Berkeley: University of California Press, 1982.

Jeri Johnson, ed. *A Portrait of the Artist as a Young Man*. World's Classics. Oxford: Oxford University Press, 2000. Full introduction and notes.

R. B. Kershner, ed. *A Portrait of the Artist as a Young Man: Case Studies in Contemporary Criticism*. Second edition. New York: Bedford/

St Martins, 2006. Cultural documents and essays illustrating different approaches.

John Paul Riquelme, ed. *A Portrait of the Artist as a Young Man: Norton Critical Edition*. New York: W. W. Norton, 2006. Includes valuable documentation and critical essays. Uses the text as edited by Gabler.

Ulysses

Don Gifford. *'Ulysses' Annotated*. Berkeley: University of California Press, 1989. Page-by-page annotations; not entirely reliable.

Jeri Johnson, ed. *Ulysses*. World's Classics. Oxford: Oxford University Press, 1993. Full editorial commentary and notes; prints the original 1922 text, which contains numerous errors and is not very pleasant to read.

Declan Kiberd, ed. *Ulysses: Annotated Student Edition*. London: Penguin, 1992. Useful notes; uses the 1960 Bodley Head text, which has many errors.

Wolfhard Steppe with Hans Walter Gabler. *A Handlist to James Joyce's 'Ulysses'*. New York: Garland, 1986. A computer-generated concordance, produced in conjunction with the 1984 edition of *Ulysses*.

Weldon Thornton. *Allusions in 'Ulysses': An Annotated List*. Chapel Hill: University of North Carolina Press, 1968.

Finnegans Wake

Adaline Glasheen. *Third Census of 'Finnegans Wake': An Index of Characters and Their Roles*. Berkeley: University of California Press, 1977. A spirited directory of people's names in the *Wake*.

Clive Hart. *A Concordance to 'Finnegans Wake'* (1963). Mamaroneck, NY: Paul P. Appel, 1974. Lists not only all the 'words' of *Finnegans Wake* but also parts of words and suggested words.

Roland McHugh. *Annotations to 'Finnegans Wake'* (1980). Third edition. Baltimore: Johns Hopkins University Press, 2006. Gathers together the interpretations of many scholars in a handy layout.

Louis O. Mink. *A 'Finnegans Wake' Gazetteer*. Bloomington: Indiana University Press, 1978. A detailed guide to place names in the *Wake*.

Other works by Joyce

Occasional, Critical and Political Writing, ed. Kevin Barry. World's Classics. Oxford: Oxford University Press, 2000.

Poems and *Exiles*, ed. J. C. C. Mays. London: Penguin, 1992.

Selected Letters, ed. Richard Ellmann. London: Faber, 1975.

Stephen Hero, ed. Theodore Spenser, John J. Slocum and Herbert Cahoon. New York: New Directions, 1955.

Critical Studies

General

Hugh Kenner. *Dublin's Joyce* (1955). New York: Columbia University Press, 1987. A classic study, lively and tendentious.

Hugh Kenner. *Joyce's Voices*. London: Faber, 1978. A readable account of the indeterminacies of narrative voice.

Fritz Senn. *Joyce's Dislocations: Essays on Reading as Translation*. Ed. John Paul Riquelme. Baltimore: Johns Hopkins University Press, 1984. Essays by one of the best readers of Joyce.

Fritz Senn. *Inductive Scrutinies: Focus on Joyce*. Ed. Christine O'Neill. Baltimore: Johns Hopkins University Press, 1995. More of Senn's close and illuminating readings.

Dubliners

Margot Norris. *Suspicious Readings of Joyce's 'Dubliners'*. Philadelphia: University of Pennsylvania Press, 2003.

Andrew Thacker, ed. *'Dubliners': Contemporary Critical Essays*. New Casebooks. Basingstoke: Palgrave Macmillan, 2006.

A Portrait of the Artist as a Young Man

Mark Wollaeger, ed. *James Joyce's 'A Portrait of the Artist as a Young Man': A Casebook*. New York: Oxford University Press, 2003.

Ulysses

Derek Attridge, ed. *James Joyce's 'Ulysses': A Casebook*. New York: Oxford University Press, 2004.

Bernard Benstock, ed. *Critical Studies on James Joyce's 'Ulysses'*. Boston: G. K. Hall, 1989.

Stuart Gilbert. *James Joyce's Ulysses* (1930). Revised edition. London: Faber, 1952; New York: Random House, 1955. Since Gilbert wrote with Joyce's assistance, this book gives a sense of how the author wanted his early readers to receive his novel.

Hugh Kenner. *'Ulysses'* (1980). Revised edition. Baltimore: Johns Hopkins University Press, 1987. Sharply observed short study.

Karen Lawrence. *The Odyssey of Style in 'Ulysses'*. Princeton: Princeton University Press, 1981. The shifts of style and their significance.

Finnegans Wake

Samuel Beckett *et al. Our Exagmination Round His Factification for Incamination of Work in Progress* (1929). London: Faber; New York: New Directions, 1972. A collection of early essays orchestrated by Joyce.

Clive Hart. *Structure and Motif in 'Finnegans Wake'*. London: Faber, 1962. Especially useful in discussing and listing repeated motifs.

Patrick A. McCarthy, ed. *Critical Essays on James Joyce's 'Finnegans Wake'*. Boston: G. K. Hall, 1992.

Margot Norris. *The Decentered Universe of 'Finnegans Wake': A Structuralist Analysis*. Baltimore: Johns Hopkins University Press, 1976. Uses theoretical models to re-examine the *Wake*.

Biography

Morris Beja. *James Joyce: A Literary Life*. Columbus: Ohio State University Press, 1992. A short, readable biography.

Richard Ellmann. *James Joyce* (1959). Revised edition. New York: Oxford University Press, 1982. Although challenged many times, this remains the fullest account of Joyce's life.

Stanislaus Joyce. *My Brother's Keeper: James Joyce's Early Years*, ed. Richard Ellmann. New York: Viking; London: Faber, 1958. First-hand reporting by Joyce's younger brother.

John McCourt. *The Years of Bloom: James Joyce in Trieste, 1904–1920*. Dublin: Lilliput, 2000. Joyce's years in Bloom described in vivid detail.

Current Journals

European Joyce Studies. Amsterdam: Rodopi. Essay collections on a variety of themes.

Hypermedia Joyce Studies. An online Joyce journal: *www.geocities.com/ hypermedia_joyce*

James Joyce Broadsheet. Reviews and short articles; published three times a year. The School of English, University of Leeds, Leeds LS2 9JT, UK

James Joyce Literary Supplement. Reviews and features, published twice a year. Department of English, PO Box 248145, University of Miami, Coral Gables, FL 33124, USA

James Joyce 'Newestlatter'. A newsletter sent to members of the International James Joyce Foundation, which also organizes a symposium every two years. Department of English, Ohio State University, 164 W. 17th Avenue, Columbus, OH 43210, USA

James Joyce Quarterly. Scholarly articles on Joyce, with book reviews, notes and lists of recent publications. University of Tulsa, Tulsa, OK 74104, USA

Joyce Studies Annual. Published by Fordham University Press. English Department, Fordham University, Bronx, NY 10458, USA

World Wide Web

There are many websites devoted to Joyce, and most provide links to other sites. Among the most useful are:

http://english.osu.edu/research/organizations/ijjf/default.cfm The website of the International James Joyce Foundation.

www.libyrinth.com/joyce/ The Brazen Head.

www.robotwisdom.com/jaj/portal.html The James Joyce Portal, a rich set of resources collated by the myriad-minded Jorn Barger.

Audio

Dubliners, *A Portrait*, *Ulysses* and *Finnegans Wake* have all been released by Naxos AudioBooks, featuring superb readings by Jim Norton and Marcella Riordan. *Dubliners*, *A Portrait* and *Ulysses* are complete; *Finnegans Wake* is abridged by Roger Marsh; abridged versions of *Ulysses* and *A Portrait* are also available.

INDEX